Praise for *Methodist Revolutions: Evangelical Engagements of Church and World*

"A time of global pandemic is a critical moment to consider who we are called to be as people of the Wesleyan tradition. This thoughtful and courageous expression of faith grounds us in our historical journey of seeking holiness, revival, reform, and revolution but does not allow us to be comfortable in our past. Reminding us of how we have been the Church, flaws and all, our friends now call us to be the Church of the present into the future God has for us and, more important, for the world and all God's creation. The transformation God yearns for the world must also be our transformation. This inspired gift of profound theological reflections with hope engages heart and mind in discerning God's will in solidarity with God and with those on the margins of life."—**Bishop Minerva G. Carcaño, Western Jurisdiction, San Francisco Episcopal Area, The United Methodist Church**

"In a world challenged by ecological crises, political upheavals, and human fragmentations, a group of global Wesleyan scholars provide us with incredibly valuable insights of the capacity of the Wesleyan traditions in contributing to the transformation of the Church and the world through revival, reform, and revolution."—**Kah-Jin Jeffrey Kuan, President, Claremont School of Theology**

"This is a well-crafted collection of works from scholars who, out of their passion for justice, seek to rekindle a Methodist revolution that is rooted in Methodism's evangelical and socially engaged tradition on the one hand and reimagines what it means to be Methodists on the other, in the here and now. As a proud Methodist, I salute Rieger and Vaai for successfully weaving this volume together across the *moana* (ocean). It is a must-read for Methodists and those who are interested in building a just and life-affirming society."—**Nāsili Vaka'uta, Principal, Trinity Methodist Theological College, Auckland, New Zealand**

"This volume is an inspiring act of protest! It offers a rich testimony (*testari*) toward (pro) ways of life that are built upon understandings of true, lasting, and life-giving transformation in both the Church and the wider world. The authors represent a variety of contexts from around the globe. This text offers a well-researched, socially engaged, and theologically rich expression of the vibrancy of Christian life in the respective contexts. I highly recommend it."—**Dion Forster, Beyers Naudé Centre for Public Theology, University of Stellenbosch. South Africa**

"These contributors, although in different locations with different perspectives and themes, are coincident in their goal to revise and renew the Methodist tradition. They pick up today's agenda as they rethink Wesleyan heritage. One may or may not agree with every point of view expressed in these pages, but without a doubt this text offers us the possibility to debate and enrich our theological understanding, challenging us to renew and revive the role and witness of the Church for our world with critical and prophetic insight."—**Néstor O. Míguez, Emeritus Professor of Systematic Theology and Bible Studies, Buenos Aires, Argentina**

Methodist Revolutions

EVANGELICAL ENGAGEMENTS OF CHURCH AND WORLD

Joerg Rieger and Upolu Lumā Vaai

GENERAL EDITORS

Nashville

First published in 2021 by the General Board of Higher Education and Ministry, Wesley's Foundery Books imprint, under ISBN 978-1-945935-94-7.

ISBN 9781791045067

Printed in the United States of America.

Contents

Introduction

Revival, Reform, and Revolution: The Differences Matter

JOERG RIEGER AND UPOLU LUMĀ VAAI

Many Wesleyans from various backgrounds and all around the world are united in the belief that another Church and another world are not only possible but also necessary. In this belief, they find themselves in agreement with many of the so-called holiness traditions. All of these traditions, even though at times addressing matters too narrowly and at other times too triumphantly, are in agreement that the status quo in both Church and world can be improved upon significantly. The questions are not whether but how does this happen and how far does it go. Amid ongoing discussions of revivals, reforms, and revolutions (the key terms found in the subtitle of the fourteenth Oxford Institute of Methodist Theological Studies in 2018[1]), this volume argues that comprehensive transformations are under way.

Our expectations are not built on shallow optimism or widespread belief in progress; they are built on evangelical expectations and holiness

1 " 'Thy Grace Restore, Thy Work Revive': Revival, Reform, and Revolution in Global Methodism," Fourteenth Oxford Institute of Methodist Theological Studies, Pembroke College, August 12–19, 2018, Oxford, England. https://oxford-institute.org/2018-fourteenth-institute/.

histories as they have been shaped since the beginnings of evangelical holiness movements. The Gospels, in which evangelical traditions are rooted, are full of challenges to establishment religion and the status quo. In Jesus's own words, "No one sews a piece of unshrunk cloth on an old cloak; otherwise, the patch pulls away from it, the new from the old, and a worse tear is made. And no one puts new wine into old wineskins; otherwise, the wine will burst the skins, and the wine is lost, and so are the skins; but one puts new wine into fresh wineskins" (Mk. 2:21–22). In the Wesleyan traditions, salvation has to do with the transformation of Church and world here and now. In his sermon "The Scripture Way of Salvation" (on Eph. 2:8, "Ye are saved through faith," KJV), John Wesley notes that salvation in this passage is not about "the going to heaven" or "a blessing which lies on the other side of death." The salvation of which this text speaks is worked out in the world. In Wesley's own words: "'Ye *are* saved.' It is not something at a distance: it is a present thing."[2] Moreover, in the history of the holiness movements, salvation was worked out not only in the present but also in relation to the poor, whose lives were foundational in early Methodism as well as the subsequent histories of Primitive Methodism, Free Methodism, the Salvation Army, and the Church of the Nazarene, as well as various Pentecostal and Wesleyan liberation movements.[3]

It is well known, of course, that Wesleyan and holiness movements have not always lived up to this legacy. Too often, holiness was privatized, as if it were only a matter of individual performance.

---

2 John Wesley, "The Scripture Way of Salvation," in *The Bicentennial Edition of the Works of John Wesley*, vol. 2, ed. Albert C. Outler (Nashville: Abingdon, 1985), 156.

3 See Donald W. Dayton, "Good News to the Poor: The Methodist Experience after Wesley," in *The Portion of the Poor: Good News to the Poor in the Wesleyan Tradition* (Nashville: Kingswood Books, 1995), 92: "In many ways, Pentecostalism is the radicalization of the holiness impulse within the Methodist traditions, or perhaps more recently a reaction to the *embourgeoisement* of the holiness churches." For Wesleyan liberation traditions, see Joerg Rieger, *No Religion but Social Religion: Liberating Wesleyan Theology* (Nashville: Foundery Books, 2018).

Things got worse when such individual performance became a matter of adjusting to dominant rules and norms rather than the spirit of the Gospel. In these developments, images of God tended to shift as well: rather than the God of the Hebrew prophets and of Jesus preaching good news to the poor, the God of whoever was in power and of a Jesus resembling the values of dominant culture set the stage for what was considered holy.

Revival

Having grown up in German Methodism, Joerg remembers tent revivals that were led by white men wearing business suits. The typical message of these events—spoken and unspoken—tended to reaffirm the lifestyles of well-behaved Methodists, while challenging slightly rebellious youth or those who did not feel much excitement about going to church. Not only were revival and holiness a matter of conforming to existing churches and their written and unwritten rules, but that conforming was also seen as the only way to make it to heaven after death. And in order not to be accused of works-righteousness (an ever-present danger especially in Lutheran-dominated Southwestern Germany), one had to define holiness almost exclusively as going to church, reading the Bible, praying, and not overstepping predetermined boundaries identified with smoking, dancing, and going to the movies. In the Pacific, where Upolu grew up during the time of Pacific countries' and churches' move toward political and religious self-determination, the historical mainline churches in particular, including the Methodist Church, focused more on reviving the nineteenth-century missionary theologies and practices that supported a conservative kind of Christianity, controlled by powerful male elites in the churches.[4] The "heavenisation" of everything, including salvation, holiness, biblical interpretation, Jesus's life and ministry, and a strong emphasis on sin

4 Manfred Ernst, *Winds of Change: Rapidly Growing Religious Groups in the Pacific Islands* (Suva: Pacific Conference of Churches, 1994).

if anyone thought differently or outside of the moral standards of life provided by the Church, was very much the spirit of the time. Hence religious independence was just a political label that had little impact on how the Pacific churches independently ran themselves outside of the nineteenth-century colonial agenda. In other words, what was revived in these settings often was merely whatever people at the time defined as the "old-time religion," which in reality amounted to religious expressions of the fairly recent past, going back as far as the nineteenth century but rarely to the times of Jesus or even Wesley himself. Conservative misperceptions of how things supposedly were from the beginning of the world accompanied these revivals. Yet, just like the business suits worn by preachers (or the idea that women belong in the home),[5] what were revived were for the most part moments in fairly recent history, imitating rules and norms that reflected the lifestyles of the powerful and the wealthy rather than those of ordinary people.[6]

Even though the mostly conservative spirit described here has shaped much of what is associated with the term *revival*, there is another side to revival as well. Among the basic theological ideas providing more solid foundations for revivals were the revival of the spirit of the early Christians and an awakening of those contemporaries who had fallen asleep. This spirit of early Christianity could be found in specific communities, such as indigenous communities whose radical life-affirming values and spirituality enhance notions of revival, as Upolu shows in chapter 8. In societies where most people were Christian, like Wesley's England, the main target of such revivals was Christianity

---

5 Only during short stretches of time in the twentieth century were women ever able to truly stay at home, without being otherwise employed. Amanda Wilkinson, "So Wives Didn't Work in the 'Good Old Days'? Wrong," *Guardian*, April 13, 2014, https://www.theguardian.com/commentisfree/2014/apr/13/working-women-stay-at-home-wives-myths.

6 In the more radical traditions of Free Methodism in the United States, commitment to "plain dress" made the poor feel more welcome and implied that people would "dress down" when going to church. Dayton, "Good News to the Poor," 85.

itself. Going back to the sources and the roots of the Christian faith could have radical implications (the Latin word *radix* means root). Just as the Reformation had its radical wing, inspired by the Gospels, so did Methodism have radical expressions in so-called Primitive Methodism (linked to the origins of the labor movement in England) and other traditions that refused to accommodate to the dominant political, economic, and religious spirits of the age. Early Methodist revivals posed some radical challenges when they promoted women preachers, preached good news to the poor, and engaged in the practice of field preaching. The last activity, in particular, was perceived as an attack on the religious establishment and those who controlled the local parishes on whose turf these activities took place. At the same time, early Methodist efforts at field preaching have also been suspected of diffusing the people's power, maintaining the status quo, and preventing deeper, necessary transformations of the substantial inequalities and suffering in eighteenth-century England. In the first chapter of the present collection, Filipe Maia investigates the Wesleyan revival in light of this critique, reclaiming the notion of revival not only in its historical complexity but also in its theological value.

Reform

In contrast to the notion of revival and its history, the notion of reform can appear to be more open and progressive. Reform, it might be argued, is based on a general awareness that things need to change. The history of Christianity is replete with reform movements that sought the transformation of some ecclesial status quo, going back to Jesus himself and his struggles with dominant religion in his time. Nevertheless, reforms can also display self-serving tendencies, like the reform of the Church of England by Henry VIII, making possible a marital divorce, or the nineteenth-century reforms of a bourgeois liberal Protestantism that made the Gospel more palatable for a prominent segment of society. Even some of the Western colonialisms would have considered themselves inspired by concerns for reform, for example in their efforts to shape colonized people around the world in their own—seemingly enlightened—images accompanied by their languages. This problem continues in the present, as Joerg shows in chapter 5, sometimes even in the form of advocacy for others.

The deeper theological concerns of reform will, therefore, have to be reclaimed as well. One of the key insights of reform has to with the problems of institutionalized religion. Plenty of examples can be given for how religion itself becomes self-serving time and again. Such religion was a constant worry for Wesley. When reclaiming the ancient tradition of the means of grace, for instance, he was concerned about the use of these means in ways that are not conducive to their purpose, which is to strengthen the relationship of God and humanity.[7] Self-serving religion claims ritual and beliefs not in order to build relationships (a topic foundational to Joerg's work) and to affirm relationality (one of the core concerns of Upolu's work) but in order to further its own power, wielded by its representatives who claim to speak for God and by its beneficiaries and benefactors. Reform, in this context, challenges self-serving religion by putting people and religion in more productive, life-affirming relationships. In so doing, reform is inspired by Jesus's rejoinder to the religious power brokers of his day that "the sabbath was made for humankind and not humankind for the sabbath" (Mark 2:27). Many of the chapters in this volume make contributions to these kinds of reforms of status quo religion in their own ways. Even the hotly debated matter of how to relate with LGBTQ+ people in the United Methodist Church appears in new light, as Keegan Osinski argues in her chapter on the "circumcision of the heart," which may well be the ultimate Pauline and Wesleyan image of reform.

---

7 John Wesley, "The Means of Grace," in *The Bicentennial Edition of the Works of John Wesley*, vol. 1, ed. Albert C. Outler (Nashville: Abingdon, 1984), 381, notes about the means of grace that "if they do not actually conduce to the knowledge and love of God they are not acceptable in his sight."

Revolution

Reclaiming revival and reform ultimately leads to fresh perspectives on the notion of revolution, which is rarely considered in its theological implications. Revolutions are not returns to earlier stages of supposed bliss, nor are they mere transformations of some status quo for slightly better results. In other words, they are neither conservative fantasies of revivals of the past nor progressive dreams of gradual reform. Revolutions are aimed at more profound change that may become necessary when the dominant status quo has managed to coopt even the best and most sincere efforts at revival and reform. This may sound extreme, but it touches on core theological commitments that can be found in various Wesleyan, evangelical, liberation, and holiness traditions. At the heart is a profound and robust notion of sin—one of the few points where Wesley was in explicit agreement with the Calvinist tradition.[8] Sin, in many of these traditions, is the fundamental rupture of human relationships with God, which leads as well to the rupturing of human relationships, personal as well as public, individual as well as structural. Any sinful state of total depravity cannot be remedied by reform, and even revival may not be enough, especially when sin leads to the destruction of the lives of communities and the planet and the oppression of the many by the few—topics that are addressed in this volume.

Yet unlike the Calvinist solution that leaves dealing with the problem of sin to God's election and predestination, Wesleyan holiness theology puts up an all-out fight against sin in all its expressions, inviting and encouraging anyone and everyone to harness the power of God to turn things around. The tangible conversion of sinners that is the result of this fight against sin must be considered nothing short of

8 In his 1744 *Minutes of Some Late Conversations*, Wesley notes that Methodists may come "to the very edge of Calvinism": "(1.) In ascribing all good to the free grace of God. (2.) In denying all natural free-will, and all power antecedent to grace. And, (3.) In excluding all merit from man." John Wesley, *The Works of the Rev. John Wesley*, ed. Thomas Jackson, 3rd ed. (London: Wesleyan Methodist Book Room, 1872; repr. Peabody, MA: Hendrickson, 1986), 8:285.

revolutionary, as it turns on its head not only private lives but also the overbearing and structural powers of sin, which all too often present themselves as the power of the status quo. In its Hebrew roots (*shubh*), conversion literally means turning around, from walking in one direction under the influence of sin to walking in the opposite direction under the influence of grace. Can there be a more revolutionary move than this?

How far does such revolution go? Where the modern study of religion and much of the modern practice of religion (in many of its varieties) tends to limit things to the individual, Wesley never buys into modern distinctions of public and private. For both Wesley and his brother Charles, there can be no religion but social religion, and there is no holiness but social holiness.[9] By this, they do not only mean that Christianity has to be practiced in community with other Christians; more poignantly, they mean that Christianity has to be practiced in public and in the world. The purpose of making disciples—of organizing people to follow Jesus, to use the language of contemporary social movements—is ultimately "for the transformation of the world," as the current mission statement of the United Methodist Church claims.[10] In other words, God's revolution knows no limits, and why should it? Why should God's revolution be limited to what is commonly defined as religion or to individuals and their private lives? Why should it even be limited to human communities and their concerns? Already Wesley

---

9 "The gospel of Christ knows of no religion, but social; no holiness but social holiness." And "Christianity is essentially a social religion, and to turn it into a solitary one is to destroy it." The first statement is from John and Charles Wesley, "List of Poetical Works," in *Works of the Rev. John Wesley*, 14:321. The second statement is from John Wesley, "Upon Our Lord's Sermon on the Mount: Discourse the Fourth," in *Bicentennial Edition of the Works of John Wesley*, 1:533. For a more detailed interpretation, see Joerg Rieger, *No Religion but Social Religion*, vii–x.

10 *The Book of Discipline of the United Methodist Church* (Nashville: The United Methodist Publishing House, 2016), paragraph 120, p. 93, states: "The mission of the Church is to make disciples of Jesus Christ for the transformation of the world."

began to understand that God's revolution extends not only to all of humanity (a crucial insight, no doubt) but also to all of creation.[11] The chapters in this volume explore and expand these sensitivities further, and we invite our readers to join us in this work.

Chapters

The chapters in this book seek to reclaim and deepen Wesleyan and holiness traditions of revival, reform, and revolution. They are in conversation with developments in recent decades that have rekindled broader perspectives that push beyond reductionistic focuses on individuals, closed communities, or particular Church bodies. They test the hope of the Gospel that is at the heart of the Methodist, evangelical, Holiness, and liberation traditions, and they look for it in concrete transformations in various parts of society and the world. Several chapters had as their origin a particularly productive workgroup at the Oxford Institute in which both editors participated, and other chapters were added in order to broaden the horizons further.

The first part of the book offers two significant historical perspectives. In chapter 1, Filipe Maia engages the much-discussed thesis that early Methodism stifled a revolution in England. In the process, he reclaims the practice of field preaching as a significant part of Wesleyan radicalism, interpreting it as a way of reclaiming the commons over and against dominant economic interests of his day. In chapter 2, Helmut Renders offers a theological account of revolution that deepens the understanding of the term by connecting it with the traditional notion of reconciliation. His examination of a particular theological development in Brazilian Methodism offers insights for Wesleyan traditions everywhere, deepening our understanding of the term *revolution* as a theological category.

11 See for instance, John Wesley, "The General Deliverance," in *Bicentennial Edition of the Works of John Wesley*, 2:437–50.

The second part of the book addresses contemporary challenges that have the potential to make or break the Church. Keegan Osinski, in chapter 3, develops a queer reading of one of Wesley's early key sermons. Thinking about the "circumcision of the heart" from LGBTQ+ perspectives is a powerful move that makes a seminal contribution to Wesleyan, holiness, and liberation traditions. At stake is not merely the inclusion of those on the margins, but also a reclaiming of our traditions that can only happen from the margins—combining revival, reform, and revolution. Chapter 4, by Pablo Guillermo Oviedo, presents an Argentinean account of how in the Wesleyan tradition relations to other people and to the divine Other can never be separated. These relationships help us develop a deeper sense for the nature of grace, one of the key terms in Wesleyan, evangelical, holiness, and liberation traditions, with profound implications for the life of the Church. Joerg Rieger's chapter 5 develops further the significance of grace in the engagements of the pressures of life, which were typical locations of the early Wesleyan and holiness traditions and which are being reclaimed today. In the process, solidarity emerges as a theological category that is not commonly used but is necessary for shedding light on a little-understood but central aspect of the Wesleyan ethos.

The final part of the book is dedicated to ecological perspectives. Timothy R. Eberhart presents a challenge to the global Methodist Church to strengthen its engagement with sustaining the planetary household not only through conversation with non-Christian environmental movements but also by refreshing the unique correlation of holiness movements and environmental protection. R. Simangaliso Kumalo and Kisitu Gyaviira bring to light the critical role of the Methodist Church in South Africa to find a radical approach in addressing the acute state of environmental degradation in their country. The authors argue that the Wesleyan ethic of care enriched by African environmentally friendly indigenous spirituality and values provides the relevant tools for addressing our global ecological plight. Upolu Lumā Vaai closes the volume with a radical call for a Methodist ecological revolution to assist in creating an alternative development story. He proposes an eco-relational theology rooted in both the Wesleyan and the Pacific concepts of relationality, an approach that might be disturbing to dominant Wesleyan traditions, to critically address a culture of ecological death posed by the neoliberal capitalist development paradigms that have led to the cry from the many Pacific grassroots communities that "others are enjoying life from our death."

The chapters of this book, written with particular contexts and struggles in mind, speak to the bigger challenge of the Wesleyan and holiness traditions for our age. If religion is indeed always social, as Wesley realized, its practitioners need to come to terms with the challenges of their times and places in order to become part of the transforming work of God. Just as there can be no nonrevolutionary Gospel, there can be no nonrevolutionary Methodism.

Joerg Rieger and Upolu Lumā Vaai, Pentecost 2020

PART ONE

Historical Perspectives

CHAPTER ONE

The Rise of the Common

Spiritual Revival and Political Revolution in the Wesleyan Movement

Filipe Maia

Keywords: field preaching, Kingswood colliers, revival, Elie Halévy, John Wesley, Industrial Revolution

Introduction

This essay offers a reading of the thesis that the Methodist revival stifled the revolutionary fervor of the English working class, an argument first introduced by Elie Halévy and expanded by E. P. Thompson. Focusing its attention on field preaching, this essay reassesses Halévy's thesis by portraying the practice as a public performance that imbricated the Methodist revival in the labor political agitation of the period. The essay suggests that we consider the performative dimension of field preaching as a mode of occupying and reclaiming the common space.

An earlier version of this chapter was presented at the Oxford Institute of Methodist Theological Studies in Oxford, England, 2018. The author would like to thank the institute's participants and the editors of this volume for their feedback.

The occupation of the fields with the public proclamation of the Gospel message constituted Methodism as a revival of the common.

Contextual Considerations

The coal mining town of Kingswood is known as one of the epicenters of Methodism, but in the first half of the eighteenth century the city was most famous for its "ungovernable" atmosphere and for numerous labor uprisings.[1] On October 1738, for example, a price dispute broke out among mine owners who decided to cut the salaries of the colliers to offset their financial losses. The reaction from workers was swift and strong: local newspapers reported that colliers performed a "general rampage through the neighbourhood which lasted for four days."[2] Not long after this incident, the town hosted a young preacher who gathered the colliers in the open fields. George Whitefield, who had "long since yearned toward the poor colliers," saw the crowd as "sheep having no shepherd" and stood upon a mount to address them.[3] Kingswood, so accustomed to the colliers' riots, became the center of a revival that grew out of the experience of field preaching.

It is customary in Methodist studies to present these two scenes—political riots and revival meetings—as running in opposite directions. The French historian Elie Halévy gave classic contours to the thesis when he argued that the Wesleyan movement precluded a violent revolution in England allowing, in its stead, for a peaceful transition to the industrial age. The consensus in studies gravitating around Halévy is

1 Robert Malcolmson, "'A Set of Ungovernable People': The Kingswood Colliers in the Eighteenth Century," in *An Ungovernable People: The English and Their Law in the Seventeenth and Eighteenth Centuries*, ed. John Brewer and John Styles (New Brunswick, NJ: Rutgers University Press, 1980), 85–127.

2 Malcolmson, "'Set of Ungovernable People,'" 116.

3 George Whitefield, *George Whitefield's Journals: A New Edition Containing Fuller Material than Any Hitherto Published* (London: Banner of Truth Trust, 1960), 216.

that the "enthusiasm" of the Methodist revival interrupted a seemingly imminent social revolution.

This essay seeks to offer a different perspective into Halévy's hypothesis by relating the political energy of protest movements in eighteenth-century England to the practice of public preaching. In other words, I want to investigate the possible continuity between the colliers' riots and field preaching in Kingswood and beyond, while indicating that political agitation and religious revival form an intriguing and politically charged pair. My argument unfolds in three movements. First, I introduce and assess Halévy's thesis along with E. P. Thompson's similar suggestion that the Methodist movement had a counterrevolutionary effect in the English context. Second, I situate the practice of field preaching at the center of the Wesleyan revival and propose that we think of this category alongside—and not opposed to—the political agitation that marked the period of the Industrial Revolution. Finally, I offer some theo-political considerations about the force of assemblies of people as gatherings that ultimately reclaim access to the common space. I propose, in closing, that field preaching constituted Methodism as a revival of the common.

Opium for the Masses: The Methodist Movement

Halévy offered the initial articulation of his thesis in the 1906 essay "The Birth of Methodism in England," in which he engages a critical question: Why didn't the labor agitations of 1738 culminate in a political revolution? The argument bears a quick recital. In the context of the social displacement generated by the Industrial Revolution, the Methodist revival offered a new sense of community and of the self. Workers, dubious about how to exercise their autonomy as an emerging class, found comfort in deferring this authority to their "brethren in Christ." Moreover, the Methodist system of governance and its supervision over people's morality offered an open path for social conformity, "making increasingly possible the relatively orderly social transformation to a modern, individualistic society during the eighteenth and nineteenth centuries."[4] For Halévy, the social malaise of the 1730s heavily impacted the English working class, and Methodism gained its force and content in this context. Workers' "despair," he concludes, "was the raw material which Methodist doctrine and discipline gave shape."[5] Methodism turned despair into accommodation of a peaceful transition to a new model of society.

Throughout the twentieth century, Halévy's hypothesis stirred historical studies of the Methodist revival.[6] Perhaps the most impressive contribution to this debate is E. P. Thompson's *The Making of the English Working Class*, a classic in the history of the labor movement in England and a masterpiece of Marxist historiography. Standing in a somewhat ambiguous relation to Halévy's thesis, Thompson points out that the Methodist movement historically coincided with the period wherein workers in England came to "feel an identity of interests as

4 Bernard Semmel, *The Methodist Revolution* (New York: Basic Books, 1973), 171–72.

5 Elie Halévy, *The Birth of Methodism in England*, trans. Bernard Semmel (Chicago: University of Chicago Press, 1971), 70.

6 See Wellman Joel Warner, *The Wesleyan Movement in the Industrial Revolution* (London and New York: Longmans, 1930); Robert Featherstone Wearmouth, *Methodism and the Working-Class Movements of England, 1800–1850* (London: Epworth, 1937); Robert Featherstone Wearmouth, *Methodism and the Struggle of the Working Classes, 1850–1900* (Leicester: E. Backus, 1954); E. J. Hobsbawn, "Methodism and the Threat of Revolution in Britain," in *Labouring Men: Studies in the History of Labour* (New York: Basic Books, 1964), 23–33; W. Reginald Ward, *Religion and Society in England, 1790–1850* (London: Batsford, 1972); Semmel, *Methodist Revolution*; David Hempton, *Methodism and Politics in British Society, 1750–1850* (Stanford: Stanford University Press, 1984); David Hempton, *The Religion of the People: Methodism and Popular Religion c. 1750–1900* (London and New York: Routledge, 1996). For a summary of Halévy's impact on the study of the history of Methodism, see Bernard Semmel, introduction to Halévy, *Birth of Methodism in England*; Elissa S. Itzkin, "The Halévy Thesis: A Working Hypothesis? English Revivalism: Antidote for Revolution and Radicalism 1789–1815," *Church History* 44, no. 1 (1975): 47–56, https://doi.org/10.2307/3165098.

between themselves, and as against their rulers and employers."[7] Notably, Thompson suggests that the "minds" that became conscious of class relations had been "molded" by Methodism.[8]

For Thompson, this was a socially ambiguous process.[9] Religiously, Methodists resembled nonconformist movements, while officially being loyal to the Church of England. Socially, Methodists generally did not endorse revolutionary politics, while being complete strangers to the establishment.[10] Thompson concludes that the revival served *simultaneously* as "the religion of the industrial bourgeoisie . . . and of the wide sections of the proletariat."[11] If, on the one hand, the poverty of the Methodists made them an antiestablishment movement, the revival's religious tenets closed the path for a social revolution. Furthermore, the Wesleyan emphasis on a gradual dimension of the *via salutis* encouraged a submissive attitude that led workers to accept and adapt to the "industrial wilderness" they were thrown into.[12] With a nod to Max Weber, Thompson affirms that the Methodist discipline and work ethic was the bridge connecting religious revival and political assimilation.[13]

Despite different emphases and divergent ideologies, historians of Methodism seem to agree on this basic tenet: the morality engendered by the Methodist revival distanced England from political radicalism—revival and revolution move in different directions. Historian David Hempton has extensively tracked this debate and offers an important summary of this consensus:

---

7 E. P. Thompson, *The Making of the English Working Class* (New York: Vintage, 1966), 11.

8 Ibid., 194.

9 For a compelling study on Thompson's ambivalent relationship to Methodism and how it stemmed from his methodological commitment to dialectic, see Hempton, *Religion of the People*, 169.

10 Thompson, *Making of the English Working Class*, 351.

11 Ibid., 355.

12 Ibid., 353.

13 See ibid., 401.

> According to Halévy, the evangelical movement imbued 'the élite of the working class, the hard-working and capable bourgeois . . . with a spirit from which the established order had nothing to fear. . . .' To this, Thompson added the idea that Methodism served as a displacement of energy away from temporal objectives into the demands of the chapel community. . . . Moreover, Methodism's work discipline . . . was the perfect foundation for industrial capitalism. Any remaining chinks in the conservative armour of Wesleyanism were sealed by the indoctrination of children, Bunting's preachers, and the expulsion of dissidents. Hence, any contribution Methodism may have made to popular politics through education and organization was incidental to its main role in the experience of working people.[14]

Fairly disappointed by the terms of the debate, Hempton argues that discussion over the revolutionary or counterrevolutionary force of Methodism often obscures the attention to regional and local forms of Methodism and the vast diversity of the movement.[15] He believes that modest claims about the impact of Methodism in industrial capitalism are closer to reality: "In this kind of environment, Methodism was at once a statement of lower middle-class independence from Anglican and gentry control, and the creator of an alternative synthesis of work, community and religious experience."[16] Hempton correctly suggests that analysts of the Methodist movement too quickly fall into the Weberian hypothesis and its tendency to portray religion as a unilateral force that favors the status quo. The view is well known: religion engenders a particular ethic, and society succumbs to it even as it rejects the religious tenet that underlined it. In the case of Methodism, the focus is therefore on the religious dimension of the revival: its class meetings,

---

14 Hempton, *Methodism and Politics in British Society*, 231.

15 Ibid., 11.

16 Ibid., 234.

its doctrine of gradual perfection, and so on.[17] To the contrary, Hempton shows several instances in which "popular evangelicalism had the capacity to act as a radical and unsettling force."[18] Methodism, in particular, "may be seen more as an expression of social radicalism than a reinforcement of *ancien régime* control."[19]

Hempton's observations may not solve the century-old dispute over Halévy's thesis, but it may offer a new perspective for considering the political impact of the Methodist movement, particularly as we consider the ties between revival and political agitation. Rather than presuming that religious movements function at the level of morality, this new perspective prioritizes the public performance of religion.[20] With this in mind, let us now return to Halévy's hypothesis by looking at an important concession made by Thompson: "Methodism . . . did offer to the uprooted and abandoned people of the Industrial Revolution some kind of community to replace the older community-patterns which were being displaced. . . . Men and women felt themselves to have some *place* in an otherwise hostile world when within the Church."[21] What place was this? What space did Methodism offer to the uprooted workers of the British Industrial Revolution? The historians of Methodism seem to direct our attention to one place—the open fields. Halévy,

17 Hempton gives credit to Thompson for his capacity to investigate the Methodist *experience* and how it impacted labor dynamics in England, instead of paying exclusive attention to the Methodist work ethic. This puts some distance between Thompson and Weber, who "confined [himself] to explaining why puritanical forms of religion had appealed almost exclusively to the middling sort with economic aspirations." Hempton, *Religion of the People*, 4.

18 Ibid., 6–7.

19 Ibid., 8.

20 In Methodist theological studies, Joerg Rieger has challenged the assumption that the Christian faith is a matter of "religion" or "morality." See Rieger, *Grace under Pressure: Negotiating the Heart of the Methodist Traditions* (Nashville: General Board of Higher Education and Ministry, The United Methodist Church, 2011).

21 Thompson, *Making of the English Working Class*, 379.

offering what to him is the ultimate proof of the Methodist conservative bent, takes us there:

> Even today, whenever a Methodist preacher brings a popular audience together at a street corner to read the Bible, sing hymns, and pray in common, whenever he induces a "revival" of mysticism and religious exaltation . . . the great movement of 1739 is being repeated. . . . A force capable of expending itself in displays of violence or popular upheavals assumes, under the influence of a century and a half of Methodism, the form least capable of unsettling a social order founded upon inequality of rank and wealth.[22]

We must pay close attention to the connection Halévy is making: the scene of public preaching is for him a waste of revolutionary energy. A radical movement could not subsist in England because its forces were being depleted by the public gatherings of the Methodist crowds. This assembly could never unsettle the social order of inequality. Halévy's text, however, points to something else: "At the beginning of 1739, the crisis was raging in [Yorkshire] . . . and it was the generally prevailing poverty that enabled Ingham, a former Oxford Methodist . . . , to produce a revival."[23] Halévy is quick to say: Benjamin Ingham "preached in the open air," again centering our attention at the public performance of the revival. But then came the winter food shortage: "Wheat being extremely expensive, the lower orders rose to seize the wheat which they were unable to buy."[24] Halévy's conclusion is that these "were favorable circumstances for the demonstration of extreme religious ardor."[25]

The reader is expected to assume that food shortage and famine are "favorable circumstances" for a religious revival, but Halévy omits an explanation of how these are also the circumstances that generated

---

22 Halévy, *Birth of Methodism in England*, 76.

23 Ibid., 71.

24 Ibid.

25 Ibid.

the riots and pillaging he describes. Kingswood is the paradigmatic case for him: Methodism found there a "mass of workingmen as savage, as degraded . . . [and] at the same time accessible to explosions of collective enthusiasm."[26] The widespread social malaise was both the cause for the riots and for the revival, but why did one mode of public gathering lead to social unrest while the other led to accommodation?

Halévy has an answer: the masses that "huddled about industrial centers" were an "ignorant mass, not capable of foreseeing and, by themselves, deciding the direction in which their enthusiasm will go."[27] These crowds of workers were no doubt restless, but their ignorance was maneuvered and took the content the bourgeoisie wanted to give it: "a religious and conservative form."[28] At this point in his argument, Halévy seemingly neglects his own claim that the public display of religious enthusiasm haunted the bourgeoisie.[29] He has embraced the thesis that field preaching came to appease the masses while overlooking that the very crowds that gathered for the Methodist revival were rioting for food in 1739. Is the violence of popular upheavals generated by the revival that much different from the crowd's rising up to "seize the wheat which they were unable to buy"?

Thompson too directs his attention to the scene of public preaching in his closing remarks about Methodism. In his case, the scene offers the most "interesting" reason as to why the working class was so attracted to Methodism:

> Charles Kingley's epithet, "the opium of the masses," reminds us that many working people turned to religion as a "consolation," even though the dreams inspired by Methodist doctrine were scarcely happy. The methods of the revivalist preachers were noted for their emotional violence. . . . And the open-air crowds and early congregations of Methodism were also noted

26 Ibid.

27 Ibid., 75.

28 Ibid.

29 Ibid., 72–74.

> for the violence of their "enthusiasm." . . . Southey, indeed, suggested that revivalism was akin to Mesmerism: Wesley "had produced a new disease, and he accounted for it by a theological theory instead of a physical one."[30]

Once again, the violence of the revival is contrasted with political radicalism. In a paragraph that speaks of opium and disease, an intriguing symptom in Thompson's statement is the association between the violence of the revival and social conservatism.[31] Like Halévy prior to him, Thompson thinks that enthusiasm is anemic compared to revolutionary fervor. Field preaching offers the most interesting explanation for the appeal that Methodism had for the English working class, and yet the violence of the enthusiasm displayed therein is just another proof of the revival's utmost pacifying force.

As historians of Methodism converge at the scene of field preaching, we encounter the moment of instability in Halévy's thesis. This unsettling point in the argument may grant us the space to offer our own question, which holds its own hypothesis: Might the scene of field preaching help us see the Methodist revival not as the antidote for a social revolution but as the very public performance of revolutionary fervor?

"A Strange Way of Preaching"

Let us now return to the scene of the riots in Kingswood. Historians of the period agree that government presence and law enforcement were scarce in several regions in England, particularly in and around forest areas. Kingswood was exemplary of this, a place with a reputation for "independence and rebelliousness," possibly the most riotous laboring group between the 1720s and the 1750s, according to historian Robert

30 Thompson, *Making of the English Working Class*, 380.

31 In fact, the images collected by Thompson seem to disagree: if revivalism was in fact opium (a painkiller), John Wesley could not have produced a new disease, only helped spread its relief.

Malcolmson.[32] According to him, the town was decidedly ungovernable: "By the mid-1720s it seems that the colliers had already acquired a reputation for a strong sense of corporate identity and effective collective action," which included the request of support from other protest movements in the area.[33] Since 1727, colliers organized several riots against two acts of Parliament that sought to establish a turnpike in the Bristol area that would authorize the charging of tolls on roads leading to and from the area. Colliers vehemently opposed the measures and brought mayhem by destroying the tolls and interrupting the supply of coal going into Bristol.[34] More than a sheer desire for destruction, what colliers rioted "against [was] the authority that had not fulfilled the people's expectations of it."[35] As Adrian Randall indicates, the struggle against tolls exposed the Kingswood colliers to the core of England's political establishment: "Turnpikes . . . were seen to emanate from that political elite with access to Westminster who were thereby able to privatize a common asset and make money from it."[36] For the Kingswood colliers, these first experiments in privatization had to be resisted. They did so by occupying and reclaiming Kingswood's common areas.

As I indicated at the opening of this essay, a labor dispute emerged in Kingswood in the autumn of 1738. The owners of the town's coal mines entered into a price war, and as a result colliers' wages went down. "Many of the colliers . . . were determined to resist this reduction . . . [and] combined together and forced others to join them in a general stoppage of work." Authorities acted fast to fortify the city and collect incriminating evidence against the rioters. Results of the uprising are

32 Malcolmson, "'Set of Ungovernable People,'" 89. For staggering numbers of the coal business operation in Kingswood, see pp. 90–91.

33 Ibid., 93.

34 Ibid., 94.

35 Ibid., 97.

36 Adrian Randall, *Riotous Assemblies: Popular Protest in Hanoverian England* (Oxford and New York: Oxford University Press, 2006), 177.

hard to gauge, Malcolmson points out, but it is certain that the repercussions of the strike lasted until April 1739.[37]

In the midst of all this controversy, George Whitefield arrived in Bristol in February 1739 and shortly afterward preached for the first time in the open fields of Kingswood. He reported in his journal: "Blessed be the Lord that I have now broken the ice! I believe I was never more acceptable to my Master than when I was standing to teach those hearers in the open fields."[38] In the ensuing weeks, Whitefield preached to several societies in the region, but whenever he was in Kingswood he was in the open fields. His journal from the period closes with the following statement: "I hope a reformation will be carried on amongst [the colliers]. For my own part, I had rather preach the Gospel to the unprejudiced, ignorant colliers, than to the bigoted, self-righteous, formal Christians. The colliers will enter into the Kingdom of God before them."[39]

Whitefield summoned John Wesley to join him in Kingswood, claiming that a "glorious door opened among the colliers."[40] After some hesitation and only after casting lots, Wesley and his friends at the Fetter Lane Society agreed about his journey to Bristol.[41] His *Journal* prefaces the importance of this event by referencing a letter written to his father, Samuel Wesley, on the occasion of his decision to pursue a "university life" in Oxford as opposed to moving back to Epworth to take over the pastoral duties from the elder Wesley.[42] It seems that Wesley thought of his journey to Bristol as yet another decisive moment when he was cutting ties with his past and moving toward a new direction.

---

37 Malcolmson, "'Set of Ungovernable People,'" 114–16.

38 Whitefield, *Journals*, 216.

39 Ibid., 243.

40 Cited in Henry D. Rack, *Reasonable Enthusiast: John Wesley and the Rise of Methodism*, 3rd ed. (London: Epworth, 2002), 190.

41 John Wesley, "Journal: March 8–15, 1739," in *The Bicentennial Edition of the Works of John Wesley*, ed. Albert C. Outler (Nashville: Abingdon, 1984), 19:37. See n64.

42 Ibid., 19:38. See also Rack, *Reasonable Enthusiast*, 191.

Wesley reached Bristol on March 31 in time to attend Whitefield's preaching. His reaction is famous: "I could scarce reconcile myself to this *strange way* of preaching in the fields . . . having been all my life (till very lately) so tenacious of every point relating to decency and order that I should have thought the saving of souls *almost a sin* if it had not been done *in a Church*."[43] That evening, Wesley preached on the Sermon on the Mount to the Nicholas Street Society and was startled by the realization that Jesus's sermon was, after all, a "remarkable precedent of *field preaching*."[44] So, on April 2, Wesley

> submitted to "be more vile," and proclaimed in the highways the glad tidings of salvation, speaking from a little eminence in a ground adjoining to the city, to about three thousand people. The Scripture on which I spoke was this . . . : "The Spirit of the Lord is upon me, because he hath anointed me to preach the gospel to the poor. He hath sent me to heal the broken-hearted, to preach deliverance to the captives and recovery of sight to the blind, to set at liberty them that are bruised, to proclaim the acceptable year of the Lord."[45]

By the end of that month, Wesley had preached to an estimated crowd of 47,500 people in the Bristol area. His *Journal* gains intensity as he narrates the experiences of people falling to the ground and crying out to God. These "violent" demonstrations—to recall the expression from Halévy and Thompson—already raised mistrust and suspicion about the revival.[46]

Did the arrival of Methodist preachers signify the end of the revolts of the Kingswood colliers? In fact, as Malcolmson observes, their riotous nature seems to have waned in the second half of the eighteenth

43 Wesley, *Works* 19:46.

44 Ibid.

45 Ibid.

46 See, for example, Wesley's entry for April 30, 1739, where he describes how many were "offended" by these signs, including a "physician, who was much afraid there might be fraud or imposture in the case." Wesley, *Works*, 19:52.

century. He suggests that "Methodism may have introduced into Kingswood a new form of authority," which led to "Kingswood [being] tamed, and its eighteenth-century turbulence . . . succeeded by quiescence during the nineteenth century."[47] Halévy's thesis is thus vindicated: Methodism functioned in Kingswood to appease the crowds. Wesley apparently shared this vision, as he declared in 1768: "No Indians are more savage than were the colliers of Kingswood; many of whom are now humane, hospitable people full of love of God and man; quiet, diligent in business; in every state content; every way adoring the gospel of God their savior."[48]

But Wesley may have overlooked how much *he* had been transformed by field preaching and how "savage" the practice was to so many of the critics of the revival. As Joerg Rieger has pointed out, Albert Outler's suggestion that Wesley was a "folk theologian" tends to overlook the ways in which Wesley was made into the theologian he was by common folk.[49] Similarly, it bears noting that the decision to meet the colliers in the open fields proved transformative to Wesley. Richard P. Heitzenrater makes the intriguing, though brief, suggestion that it was the experience of field preaching that shifted Wesley's focus away from his personal anguish around assurance of faith to a "more public and evangelical sense of vocation."[50] On April 4, 1739, Wesley wrote in his journal what amounts to a theological defense of field preaching: "How dare any man deny this to be (as to the substance of it) a means of grace, ordained by God?"[51] Heitzenrater's suggestion seems all the more valid in light of this: within days of his first contact with the open

---

47 Malcolmson, "'Set of Ungovernable People,'" 127.

48 Cited in ibid., 125.

49 Rieger, *Grace under Pressure*, 39; Joerg Rieger, *No Religion but Social Religion: Liberating Wesleyan Theology* (Nashville: Foundery Books, 2018), 12.

50 Richard P. Heitzenrater, *The Elusive Mr. Wesley*, 2nd rev. ed (Nashville: Abingdon, 2003), 102. See also Richard P. Heitzenrater, *Mirror and Memory: Reflections on Early Methodism* (Nashville: Kingswood Books, 1989), 133.

51 Wesley, *Works*, 19:47.

fields of Kingswood, Wesley was thinking of field preaching within the category of means of grace.

Wesley's shift toward a more public understanding of his ministry immediately placed him at the center of England's social tensions. Field preaching was not illegal in England, but it was irregular.[52] In 1739 Whitefield was the first to face problems with the chancellor of the diocese of Bristol.[53] His response was somewhat standard for Methodism: field preaching was a way to appeal to a large sector of the populace that was excluded from the churches, and the fruits of the practice proved its divine nature.[54] Wesley used similar arguments in his engagement with Bishop Butler, also from Bristol, with whom he may have met on at least three occasions to discuss his case.[55] Edmund Gibson, bishop of London between 1720 and 1748, was initially prone to favor the Methodist movement but later defended the thesis that field preaching was in fact illegal.[56]

As Hempton indicates, the Methodist revival "appeared to undermine traditional authority" through its critique of the clergy, but also because its endorsement of "itinerant, lay, and female preachers crossed traditional boundaries of hierarchy, law, sex, age, wealth, education and religious vocation."[57] Field preaching, in particular, was met with direct resistance from the top ranks of society: "Anti-Methodist rioting was seen from one perspective as an instrument of social control."[58] The following from the Cork Baptist Church Book cements the notion that opposition to field preaching was a necessary mechanism for social control:

52 Richard P. Heitzenrater, *Wesley and the People Called Methodists*, 2nd ed. (Nashville: Abingdon, 2013), 109.

53 Whitefield, *Journals*, 213–22.

54 See ibid., 222.

55 Rack, *Reasonable Enthusiast*, 208–9.

56 See Hempton, *Religion of the People*, 147.

57 Ibid., 149.

58 Ibid.

> From their first appearance the novelty of preaching in the fields, their seeming zeal and disinterestedness gained them a multitude of hearers. . . . The multitudes of all ranks of people that resorted to the fields to hear them gave range to the magistrates and 'tis not improbable but the mob were countenanced in disturbing their assemblies, 'tis certain that such kind of assemblies are subject to tumults . . . , yet the laws do not protect such wild promiscuous assemblies. Besides there was some reason to think that the working people were interrupted from their labour and while out of pretense religion they ran after such preachers their families at home were left destitute.[59]

In this blend of religious and social attack, it is noteworthy that field preaching was perceived as a threat to the work ethic and that gathering in the open fields was associated with idleness. While legal disputes were intense, much of the opposition to field preaching exposed class bias against Methodism.[60]

To audiences accustomed to seeing assemblies of working-class people as a sign of rebellion, the crowds assembled by the Methodist revival seemed just another threat to established authorities. Historian John Walsh highlights that the "resentment of gentry and clergy [against Methodism] is not hard to explain. . . . They feared it as a challenge to public order and to the authority of their class."[61] Henry Rack reiterates Walsh's observation: "Whatever the truth of . . . speculative Weberian notions about the effects on the capitalist spirit, contemporaries saw [Methodists'] social disruptiveness."[62] Historian Nicholas Rogers confirms that "crowd interventions were a constituent element in the rich

59 The Cork Baptist Church Book, 1653–1875. Cited in Hempton, *Religion of the People*, 153–54.

60 See Hempton, *Religion of the People*, 149.

61 John Walsh, "Methodism and the Mob in the Eighteenth Century," in *Popular Belief and Practice: Papers Read at the Ninth Summer Meeting and the Tenth Winter Meeting of the Ecclesiastical History Society*, Studies in Church History 8 (Cambridge: Cambridge University Press, 1972), 218.

62 Rack, *Reasonable Enthusiast*, 280.

and ramified demotic political culture of the Georgian era [ca. 1714–1830]" and that these interventions occupied a "contested terrain in which power, ideology, and class interest intersected."[63] This must be clear: field preaching placed the Methodist revival right at the center of this terrain and helped expose class tensions in English society.

Field preaching indelibly links the Wesleyan revival to the political agitation of the Industrial Revolution. Crowds of riotous workers and crowds of enthusiast believers performed the same act of placement for a displaced population. To recall Thompson's thesis: "Methodism . . . did offer to the uprooted and abandoned people of the Industrial Revolution . . . some *place* in an otherwise hostile world." Yet it is not just that workers found their place in the Methodist revival, but also fundamentally that the Methodist revival found its place in the common space already opened up by the political riots of the emerging working class.

Kingswood had a place for the Methodist preachers because the open fields had been the place of the colliers. What many perceive as the sign of the colliers' accommodation to the status quo may well have been their ongoing resistance to the establishment as they continued to claim the open fields as their field of action. What some see as the success of Methodism in taming the colliers might have been the success of the colliers in making Wesleyan theology a true form of political theology of the commons—a theology of the open fields.

A Theology of the Commons

The perspective on the political impact of the Methodist revival afforded by the scene of public preaching gains force when one considers crowds as political agents and not mere spectators. Theorist Judith Butler insists that politics not only is the bureaucratic distribution of political functions but also fundamentally is about the performance of

63 Nicholas Rogers, *Crowds, Culture, and Politics in Georgian Britain* (New York: Oxford University Press, 1998), 17–18.

political acts.[64] To assess the political impact of the Methodist revival one must consider the political force of such acts. The practice of field preaching imparted a radical edge to the Methodist revival. This rise of the commons offers an entryway into the political theology of the Wesleyan movement and its own form of theology of the crowds.

The Methodist experience is entangled in the movement of the crowds. Though he claimed that the Kingswood colliers had been appeased by the Methodist revival, Wesley was constantly having to handle the tensions created by field preaching, tensions that the Methodist movement only intensified. In his essay "A Farther Appeal to Men of Reason and Religion," Wesley takes on a critic of Methodism who was especially concerned about the tumult generated by field preaching. Wesley rejects the legal argument against the practice, but his adversary suggested that field preaching was not only illegal but also dangerous. The charge was openly political: "[Field preaching] may be attended with mischievous consequences. It may give advantages to the enemies of the established government. It is big with mischief."[65] Even if "Methodists themselves are a harmless and loyal people," field preaching remained a useful site for "disloyal and seditious persons."[66]

The argument was compelling, and Wesley was obliged to concede that crowds might become tumultuous. He was, however, willing to say that the revival may in fact be an agent of public disruption. Wesley, the leader who professed to be so "tenacious of every point relating to decency and order," ultimately granted that field preaching was a disturbance of public order much like the apostles disturbed the peace of the Roman Empire—an intriguing correlation established by Wesley.[67] One may glimpse at his theological understanding of the political

64 Judith Butler, *Notes toward a Performative Theory of Assembly* (Cambridge, MA: Harvard University Press, 2018).

65 John Wesley, "A Farther Appeal to Men of Reason and Religion," in *The Works of John Wesley*, ed. Thomas Jackson (Grand Rapids, MI: Zondervan, 1958), 8:115.

66 Ibid.

67 *Works*, 19:46.

force of crowds of people: "Although what we preach is the gospel of peace, yet if you will violently and illegally hinder our preaching, must this not create disturbance?"[68] The crowds gathered in the open fields were helping Wesley turn the tables: the disturbance generated by field preaching was a fruit of his adversaries' own incapacity to witness the public appearance of the Gospel. Field preaching would indeed be a disturbance as long as the order of society was unjust.

Wesley goes on to insist that field preaching was not part of his own design: "Field-preaching was therefore a sudden expedient, a thing submitted to, rather than chosen; and therefore submitted to, because I thought preaching even thus, better than not preaching at all."[69] The constant reference to the spontaneous nature of field preaching is important for Wesley as he seems to guard himself against the claim that causing a public scene was his intention all along. To address criticisms against the "manner of our preaching," he uses all sorts of explanations, from doctrinal issues to climatic factors.[70] But his meticulous reasoning comes to a halt when he introduces his adversary to the "awful sight" of a multitude gathering in the open fields of Kingswood. The prose of "Farther Appeal" breaks up to give room to hymnody: "[The crowds] were waiting upon God, while

> They stood, under an open air adored
> The God who made both air, earth, heaven, and sky."[71]

Wesley says in his heart: "This . . . is no other than the house of God! This is the gate of heaven!"[72] Wesley, who once cautioned his preachers against excessive field preaching, is shown here appreciating the fact that the open fields are indeed the house of God.[73] His awe before

68 *Works* (Jackson), 8:121.

69 Ibid., 8:113.

70 Ibid., 8:112.

71 Ibid.

72 Ibid.

73 For a discussion of Wesley's advice to limit field preaching, see Heitzenrater, *Wesley and the People Called Methodists*, 165–66.

the crowds bespeaks his realization that the revival was politically disrupting and that this disruption was significant to the revival's understanding of the work of God.

In her book *Notes toward a Performative Theory of Assembly*, Butler suggests that the gathering of bodies—the assembly—is politically meaningful. Assemblies signify something, even when nothing is said: "Acting in concert can be the embodied form of calling into question the inchoate and powerful dimensions of reigning notions of the political."[74] For Butler, there is something transgressive—*seditious*, to recall Wesley's opponent's term—about the apparition of these bodily assemblies in the public scene, particularly when the bodies that show up are those that often disappear before the public eye: "[W]hen bodies assemble on the street, in the square, or in other forms of public space . . . they are exercising the right to appear, one that asserts and instates the body in the midst of the political field, and which . . . delivers a bodily demand for a more livable set of economic, social, and political conditions no longer afflicted by induced forms of precarity."[75] For Butler, the apparition of precarious bodies in the assembled crowd exposes the injustices of the system. These spontaneous gatherings constitute a political irruption of a power that has been repressed. The act is creative insofar as it generates conditions for the possibility of life in an environment that is stifling. Might this offer a new perspective into the assembled crowds in the open fields of Kingswood and beyond? Might the Methodist revival be another instantiation of the right to appear, performed by those living under precarious conditions?

Butler's analysis stems from the contemporary scene, an atmosphere that has been impacted by political movements occupying the public space. These movements expose and confront the injustices of our own time. Reflecting on this context, theologians Joerg Rieger and Kwok Pui-lan affirm the theological depth of the concept of the multitude and its affinity with the biblical categories of *laos* and *ochlos*, both Greek terms used by New Testament writers to designate the common

74 Butler, *Notes toward a Performative Theory of Assembly*, 9.

75 Ibid., 11.

people that constituted Jesus's movement. According to Rieger and Kwok, one does not simply join a multitude, but rather one makes the multitude.[76] As Butler argues, the common space is not a given but rather is constituted as public space as people assemble. The assembly of people makes the space into a common space; it "reconfigure[s] the materiality of public space and produce[s], or reproduce[s], the public character of that material environment."[77]

The consideration of the political force of crowds puts in check the traditional position that masses of people are often "blind," as Halévy insisted, or reactionary, as Thompson implied. With Butler's analysis of the performative power of the assembly, it is possible to suggest that political transformation and revolutionary fervor are not engendered by the morality espoused by a movement or by its bureaucratic organization. More than simply shaping a discipline favorable to the creation of a submissive worker, the Methodist revival helped to create a common space that offered home to those who had been displaced. The occupation of the commons by the crowds of Methodists "create[d] psychical and imaginary spaces so that an alternative world can be thought and experienced."[78] Before any Methodist ethic or doctrine was preached, the crowds of coal miners, artisans, women, and children spoke through their collective presence in occupying the commons.

In radical grassroots movements, the commons are open spaces, public squares, common fields, and forests that escape the logic of private ownership and top-down power hierarchies. Through its practice of field preaching, the Methodist revival took place in an already politically charged site—the open fields. This imbued the movement with a radical edge by aligning it with the movements of the dispossessed masses of English workers. Field preaching constituted the Methodist movement as a movement of the commons for the commons.

---

76 Joerg Rieger and Kwok Pui-lan, *Occupy Religion: Theology of the Multitude* (Lanham, MD: Rowman and Littlefield, 2012), 32.

77 Butler, *Notes toward a Performative Theory of Assembly*, 71.

78 Rieger and Kwok, *Occupy Religion*, 5.

Rieger and Kwok justly say: "God will not be found . . . where God can be controlled."[79] Indeed, the Methodist revival found its way to God in the uncontrollable crowds gathered in the open fields. Along with other movements, the Methodist revival reclaimed, occupied, and ultimately revived the commons. Field preaching, one could say with a nod to David Harvey, "delineate[d] liminal social spaces of possibility where 'something different' is not only possible, but foundational for the defining of revolutionary trajectories."[80] The fields of Kingswood became this liminal social space of possibility for the revival. The Methodist revival was constituted in the occupation of the commons. In Wesley's terms, it became the house of God for the people called Methodist. The space that the colliers found in Methodism was this common space—a space already known to them through decades of political agitation. What Methodism did was not so much to appease these crowds as to occupy a space they had known and to perceive in those open fields the house of God. Methodism occupied the public sphere with its proclamation of the Gospel and, in this process, allowed for the poor and working classes to perceive that indeed there was room for them in the city. The crowds that gathered to witness to the event of preaching did not simply join the Methodist movement but rather constituted Methodism as a movement of the multitudes. In a foreign territory where there is no room for public life, Methodism offered a glimpse of life in the commons, and there it found its God.

79 Ibid., 108.

80 David Harvey, *Rebel Cities: From the Right to the City to the Urban Revolution* (London: Verso, 2013), xvii.

CHAPTER TWO

Reconciliation as Deep Revolution

Atonement and the Overcoming of Enmity in a Brazilian Methodist Perspective

Helmut Renders

Keywords: reconciliation, Brazilian Methodism, mission, atonement, Social Creed, convivence, hospitality

Introduction

The phrase "reconciliation as deep revolution" unites two concepts that are often understood as contradictions. Nevertheless, the two languages or narratives from different worlds enable us to look to one another, to hear one another, and to grow with one another.

Contextual Considerations

Methodism is often understood as an extension of the Reformation narrative, which saved England from a revolution, at least from a revolution like France experienced. This is the reason why the initial title of the Oxford Institute of 2018 mentioned "reform, revival, and renewal," but not revolution.[1] Here we must ask who exactly wants to reform, revive, and renew what or whom. And although revolution may sound too strong to many, reform, revival, and renewal can sound too uncommitted and too superficial to others. Therefore, when I requested the addition of the word *revolution* to the theme of the conference, I provoked a vivid discussion. Some were not happy about my approximation of revolution and Methodism; for others, *revolution* easily connected to their experiences. For sure, Latin American Protestants have used the term to describe the importance of Jesus in and for their society, even before liberation theology occupied this linguistic territory. This happened, for example, in 1962, when the Department for Social Affairs of the Evangelical Confederation of Brazil titled its third conference in Brazil's Northeast "Christ and the Revolutionary Brazilian Process."[2]

In my request, I used the term in the tradition of this publication, sharing its interest in a Methodism that cares for the actual situation of the country and asking which of its resources may contribute to reforming the nation, especially the Church. Brazilian Methodism did this, as I want to show in this chapter, by revisiting from time to time its understanding of reconciliation, based on a specific interpretation of reconciliation as overcoming human enmity by divine friendship. In a second step, I shall connect this to the understanding of hospitality, *philoxenia*, as the churches' inner correspondence to this challenge. Not

---

1 An earlier version of this chapter was presented at the Oxford Institute of Methodist Theological Studies in Oxford, England, 2018.

2 Confederação Evangélica do Brasil, *A conferência do Nordeste: Cristo e o processo revolucionário brasileiro*, 2 vols. (Rio de Janeiro: Loqui, 1962): vol 1, *Narrativa em forma de diara de toda a semana do Nordeste*; vol 2, *Reunião de Estudos*. See also Magali Nascimento Cunha and Helmut Renders, *As igrejas e as mudanças sociais: 50 anos da conferência do Nordeste* (São Bernardo do Campo, SP: Editeo / São Paulo: ASTE, 2012). Within the theory of revolution, this is classified as a lowercase revolutionary process, focused on the creation of alternative spaces and the promotion of horizontal participative decision processes. See Thomas Nail, "Revolution,"in *Keywords for Radicals: The Contested Vocabulary of Late-Capitalist Struggle*, ed. Kelly Fritsch, Clare O'Connor, and AK Thompson (Chico, CA: AK, 2016), 376–77.

to exclude and not to deform, not to flee and not to attack to destroy, to win the other, not to struggle, seem to me a truly deep revolution. It is the reestablishment of hope for real—or deep?—transformation in a lively and dynamic context and its real-life conflicts. Is it not interesting that reconciliation, convivence, and hospitality all identify and address enmity as the key problem of society? It seems to me that this perception, throughout history, has been several times lost and found again. Some examples of today's version of enmity are hate crimes and the disqualification of people on grounds of their ethnicity, sexuality, gender, social class, or religious choices.

1888–1930: Establishing Reconciliation as Overcoming Human Enmity by Divine Friendship as a Theological Paradigm

I first became aware of the centrality of the reconciliation paradigm in classical Brazilian Methodism when I studied the Brazilian version of the Methodist Articles of Religion.[3] It occurred to me that Methodist missionaries, soon after their official arrival in 1867, initiated a revolution when they changed the second article, although it was by then already protected by the first restrictive order of the General Conference. Where the English text refers to the work of Christ as being "to reconcile His Father to us," the translation to the Brazilian Portuguese follows Paul: "to reconcile us to his Father."

At a time when slavery was still in force in Brazil, Methodist missionaries challenged it doctrinally by ruling out Anselm's theory of satisfaction and its analogy between a feudalist society and God's presence in the world. Not divine wrath, or God's enmity, had to be undone by Christ; no sacrifice was necessary to reestablish the honor of the Lord. Human enmity had to be faced and to be challenged by God's kindness

3 Helmut Renders, "To Reconcile Us to His Father": A Unique Translation of the Second Article of Religion of the Methodist Church in Brazil and Three Other Lusophone Countries," *Methodist Review* 5 (2013): 2–51.

and friendship—this idea established a doctrinal *cantus firmus* that was revisited several times in the subsequent eighty years.

The second time I realized that Brazilians did things quite differently from their mother church was again doctrinal but this time was related to ethics. No doubt, the Social Creed was an important "official document engaging the authority of the [Methodist Episcopal] Church."[4] Nevertheless, the Methodist Episcopal Church located the creed in the appendix of its Book of Discipline, the part currently referred to as the Book of Resolutions, as it contains the nonbinding but suggested ethical application of doctrine. In this location the Social Creed was still good for reform but not good enough for profound revolutionary changes and breakthroughs. Again, the Methodist Episcopal Church, South, did not embrace a mere reformist approach. Responding to the catastrophic consequences of World War I, it linked the creed directly to the committees of the Annual Conference. The creed was something to work with.

1930–71: Unfolding Reconciliation as Overcoming Human Enmity by Divine Friendship in Its Public Dimension

When the autonomy of the Brazilian Methodist Church was achieved in 1930, the new church placed the Social Creed in the constitutive part of the discipline, something that in American Methodism only happened in 1968 with the foundation of the United Methodist Church. At the same time, the church preserved the specific Brazilian change of the second Article of Religion, now protected by a restrictive order, and it still maintains this change in its Book of Discipline today. In the first thirty years of the church's existence, works by authors such as Walter Rauschenbusch were studied in Brazilian Methodism soon

4 José Miguéz Bonino, "Reflections of the Church's Authoritative Teaching on Social Questions," in *What Should Methodists Teach?*, ed. M. Douglas Meeks (Nashville: Kingswood Books, 1990), 61–62.

after their publication. His contributions concerning atonement definitely affirmed the path already chosen, introducing solidarity as a key term of his theory of atonement, replacing classic atonement theories. The point of departure for this solidarity is experience by incarnation:[5]

> How did Jesus bear sins, which he did not commit? The old theology replied, by imputation. But guilt and merit are personal. . . .
>
> Neither is it enough to say that Jesus bore our sins by sympathy. His contact with sin was a matter of experience as well as sympathy, and experience cuts deeper.[6]

A little further on, Rauschenbusch addresses forensic (as propounded by Anselm and John Calvin) and governmental (Grotius) theories of atonement.

> But, taken in connection with his life, as the inevitable climax of his prophetic career, his death had an essential place in his work of establishing solidarity and reconciliation between God and man. It was his supreme act of opposition to sin; not even the fear or the pangs of death could make him yield anything of what God had given him to hold. It was the supreme act, also, of obedience to God, to which he was moved by love to God and loyalty to his Kingdom. . . . This conception is free from the artificial and immoral elements inherent in all forensic and governmental interpretations of the atonement. It begins with the solidarity between God and Christ and

5 "None of the later theories of the atonement is taught, or even touched, in the sayings of Jesus, except perhaps at the Lord's Supper. The only clear interpretation of his death from his own mind is this, that he ranged his sufferings in line with those of the prophets. This lifts the experiences and functions of the prophets to a very high level in the redemption of mankind." Walter Rauschenbusch, *A Theology for the Social Gospel* (New York: Macmillan, 1918), 260.

6 Rauschenbusch, *Theology for the Social Gospel*, 245–46.

> proceeds to the solidarity between God and mankind. It deals with social and religious realities.[7]

Like the US and Brazilian Methodists before, Rauschenbusch argued that one key question for the testimony of the Church is its option for one or another theory of atonement. His personal emphasis on the term *solidarity*[8] was an important ingredient for those who understood reconciliation also in its horizontal or Ephesian terms, as the reconciliation between human beings as well as social, ethnic, or religious groups. So it was not by accident that the new church in 1930 created a Brazilian version of the Social Creed, which differed from its American version,[9] giving extra consideration to the situation of rural workers and the female vote—constitutionally guaranteed in Brazil in 1932.[10] These two new accents we may consider more revolutionary than reformist.

The inclusion of the Social Creed in the Brazilian Manual for Church Members in 1921 shows how the Brazilian Church understood the Social Creed as an orientation for Christian citizenship as a whole and not only as an orientation for church officials.[11] When the Methodist Episcopal Church, South, approved the autonomy of the Brazilian

---

7 Ibid., 260.

8 Rauschenbusch used the term in several senses. "We are linked in a solidarity of evil and guilt with all who have done the same before us, and all who will do the same after us. In so far then as we, by our conscious actions or our passive consent, have repeated the sins which killed Jesus, we have made ourselves guilty of his death." Ibid., 258.

9 First introduced in Brazil in 1918. See Egreja Methodista Epsicopal, Sul, *Credo Social.* Doutrinas e Disciplinas da Igreja Methodista Episcoal, Sul, 1918. Edição brasileira (São Paulo: Casa Publicadora Methodista, 1919), 404–5 [§808].

10 For all Brazilian versions of the Social Creed, see Helmut Renders, comp., *Sal da terra e luz do mundo: 100 anos do Credo Social Metodista* (São Bernardo do Campo: Editeo, 2009).

11 Paul Eugene Buyers, *Manual para os membros da Egreja Methodista* (São Paulo: Imprensa Metodista, 1921), 110–12.

Mission in 1930, the social gospel discourse was also present in the bishop's key address:

> Bishop James Cannon Junior made a discourse about "The Church and the Social Gospel." He exposed the fundamental principles of all Church activities and explained carefully the difference between a direct Gospel appeal to every individual soul and the necessary relationship of each individual to society. The principle of human brotherhood . . . should finally transform the whole human society. This principle should be applied in all industrial, international and social relations. . . . The Bishop stated that it is in fact very important and significant that the Methodist Church of Brazil showed in its first public meeting . . . emphatically its attitude in descent to the social Gospel of Jesus, putting this new Church in the front line with the best of Methodism since the days of Wesley.[12]

We do not know exactly what Bishop James Cannon Jr. wanted to say. For sure, he was very conservative and the leader of the Prohibition movement in the United States. But his affirmation that "the principle of human brotherhood . . . should finally transform the whole human society" and that "this principle should be applied in all industrial, international and social relations" cannot be restricted to Cannon's personal issue. This is the language of the social gospel. It seems to me that here the more progressive part of the Brazilian Church created a narrative in the form of a conference memory, considering the possibility that Cannon did not say all of this with this intention. In a soteriological sense, "the principle of human brotherhood" is rooted in the understanding of reconciliation as overcoming enmity by friendship. We shall see in the next section that Brazilian Methodists understood the principle literally.

---

12 Igreja Metodista do Brasil, *Actas da Comissão Constituinte* (São Paulo), August 28–September 2, 1930, 40.

Cannon's address reveals also that some work still had to be done to convince parts of Brazilian Methodism of the public extension of its theology of reconciliation. So they linked their narrative to Methodist history and qualified it as "the best of Methodism since the days of Wesley." The application of the principle of human fellowship to all imaginable expressions of the public life was rooted or anchored in the foundational myth of Methodism. What makes this text part of a project to promote deep reconciliation, however, is not merely the appeal to engage with the public with a Christian spirit. It is the "appeal to every individual soul and the necessary relationship of each individual to society." Here it is not the church as an institution, which does the public part, while church members live their faith in more or less restricted privacy. The principle of human fellowship, applied within and beyond the church, is deep reconciliation, so personal that it reaches every individual soul.

Sedimenting Reconciliation as Overcoming Human Enmity by Divine Friendship and Its Public Dimension in the Social Creed of 1971

In Brazil a more open rejection of this theological, ecclesiastical, and social project occurred within other Protestant churches, especially Baptist and Presbyterian churches and in parts of the Methodist Church, with the beginning of the dictatorship in 1964. Rauschenbusch's understanding of atonement as divine solidarity, which leads to the solidarity of the church for humankind, had anticipated what Dietrich Bonhoeffer had formulated in the 1930s: "The Church is the Church only when it exists for others."[13] By the early 1960s, the works of Bonhoeffer were widely read in Brazil, although he and Karl Barth

13 Dietrich Bonhoeffer, *Widerstand und Ergebung / Entwurf für eine Arbeit* (Gütersloh: Gütersloher Verlagshaus, 2015), 560, translation mine.

were known before.[14] His theology of discipleship was also rooted in the specific understanding of reconciliation as overcoming human enmity by God's friendship in Christ:

> How then does love conquer? By asking not how the enemy treats her but only how Jesus treated her. The love for our enemies takes us along the way of the cross and into fellowship with the Crucified. The more we are driven along this road, the more certain is the victory of love over the enemy's hatred. For then, it is not the disciple's own love, but the love of Jesus Christ alone, who for the sake of his enemies went to the cross and prayed for them as he hung there. In the face of the cross, the disciples realized that they too were his enemies and that he had overcome them by his love. It is this which opens the disciple's eyes, and enables him to see his enemy as a brother. He knows that he owes his very life to one, who thought he was his enemy, treated him as a brother and accepted him, who made him his neighbour and drew him into fellowship with himself. The disciple can now perceive that even his enemy is the object of God's love and that he stands like himself beneath the cross of Christ. God asked us nothing about our virtues or our vices, for in his sight even our virtue was ungodliness. God's love sought out his enemies who needed it, and whom he deemed worthy of it. God loves his enemies—that is the glory of his love, as every follower of Jesus knows; through Jesus, he has become a partaker in this love.[15]

---

14 Brazilian Methodists knew early what was happening in Germany. In the church's official journal, the *Expositor Cristão*, several articles referred to the conflict. See Helmut Renders, "Compromisso pastoral, clareza teológica e cidadania: a Declaração Teológica de Barmen como resultado de uma interação entre Igreja e academia teológica," *Caminhando* 14, no. 2 (2009): 109–28.

15 Dietrich Bonhoeffer, *The Cost of Discipleship*, rev. and unabridged ed., trans. R. H. Fuller with some revision by Irmgard Booth (New York: Macmillan, 1976), 166–67.

I quoted only one of the central parts, but the text contains many more such references.[16] Bonhoeffer not only reaffirmed what was already a tradition in Brazilian Methodism, but he also radicalized it, and this became relevant for Brazilian Protestants, including Methodists, in the 1960s. My point is that social responsibility among Brazilian social gospelers is part of their soteriology and understanding of reconciliation. The capacity of parts of the Methodist Church to articulate resistance and, eventually, to resist dictatorship is also manifest in its special emphasis on reconciliation as overcoming human enmity by divine friendship in its Social Creed of 1971.[17] This version of the Brazilian Social Creed was created during the worst time of the Brazilian military regime. Its vision of the public calling of the church, based on a theology of reconciliation within the enmity-friendship framework, displays a very prophetic and a very pastoral tone. When we talk about deep reconciliation in Methodist terms, we should affirm that the prophetic and pastoral dimension belong together. It is justice and mercy.[18]

In the Social Creed of 1971, reconciliation is clearly understood in Pauline and post-Pauline terms, combining Corinthians with Ephesians.[19] Reconciliation is presented here as a performative act that leads

---

16 Ibid., 45, 46, 85, 158, 164.

17 Helmut Renders, "75 anos do Credo Social brasileiro: Uma investigação da interação entre igreja e esfera pública," *Simpósio* 11, no. 1, ano XL 49 (2009): 43–65.

18 Interestingly, this is also the theological framework of John Wesley's "Thoughts upon Slavery" of 1774. He used it eight times, in sections 2.11, 4.2, 5.1, 5.3, 5.5, and 4.6 and in the parts he wrote in with Granville Sharp (1735–1813) and Antoine Bénézet (1713–64), with whom he formed a network of resistance from 1760 onward. See Helmut Renders, *John Wesley e a luta abolicionista: Com edição bilíngue dos seus Pensamentos sobre a escravidão* (São Paulo: ASTE, 2019).

19 Probably because one of its major contributors, Ely Eser Barreto César, was a trained New Testament scholar firmly rooted in the discussion of Pauline theology in a liberation perspective. See Ely Eser Barreto César, *A fé como ação na história*: *Hermenêutica do novo testamento no contexto da América Latina* (São Paulo: Paulinas, 1988).

to the vocation to share this message as an essential part of the annunciation of the Gospel. In the following quotation, bold characters identify this specific language of reconciliation.

The Social-Political and Economic Order

4. We believe that the one God was in Christ, **reconciling the world to himself** and creating a new order of things in history by forgiving the sins of men and entrusting us **with the ministry of reconciliation. . . .**

The next part, paragraph 5, explains the social impact of God's "reconciling love in Jesus Christ" as a source and model for new forms of encounters and challenges the church to understand its special call always to anticipate its own message by applying it to itself:

5. The Methodist Church in the present situation of the country and the world considers clear perception of the following realities to be particularly important for its social responsibility:

    a. God created the nations to form a universal family. **His reconciling love in Jesus Christ overcomes barriers** between brothers and **destroys every form of discrimination of human beings**. The Church is called to lead all to welcome and affirm one another as persons in all their relationships: in the family, in the neighbourhood, work, education, leisure, religion, and the exercise of political rights.
    b. **The reconciliation of the world in Jesus Christ is the source of justice, peace, and freedom among nations**; all the structures and authorities of society are called to participate in this new order. **The Church is the community that exemplifies these new relations of forgiveness, justice, and freedom**, commanding them to governments and nations as a way towards a responsible policy of cooperation and peace.

Whereas (c) identifies areas of conflict or expressions of enmity between the nations, (d) to (g)—nearly 50 percent of the text—describes poverty as a central expression of an unreconciled world.

c. **Reconciliation between nations becomes particularly urgent at a time when countries are developing nuclear, chemical, and biological weapons**, diverting vast resources from constructive purposes and putting mankind at risk.
d. **The reconciliation of man in Jesus Christ makes clear that enslaving poverty in a world of plenty is a grave violation of God's order**; the identification of Jesus Christ with the needy and the oppressed, and the priority of justice in the Scriptures, proclaim that the cause of the poor in the world is that of his disciples.
e. The poverty of an enormous part of the human family, a result of economic imbalances, unjust social structures, exploitation of the defenseless, lack of knowledge, is a grave negation of God's justice.
f. The extreme cultural, social, and economic **inequalities are a denial of justice and put peace at risk**, and urgently require appropriate intervention with effective planning to overcome them.
g. It is unjust to increase the **wealth of the rich and the power of the strong by increasing the distress of the poor** and oppressed. Programs to increase the national income should provide for an equitable distribution of resources, combat discrimination, overcome economic injustices, and free man from want.[20]

---

20 "The Methodist Church of Brazil, Social Creed, 1971," in *Statements of Faith in Modern Christianity,* vol. 3 of *Creeds and Confessions of Faith in the Christian Tradition*, ed. Jaroslav Pelikan and Valerie Hotchkiss (New Haven: Yale University Press, 2003), 735.

Read within the framework of reconciliation as a process of overcoming enmity by friendship, these affirmations emphasize a number of themes. The reasons for barriers and hostilities are overcome in Christ by his predisposition toward the world ("His reconciling love in Jesus Christ overcomes barriers"), as shown on the cross. This introduces the world to a new logic and reason ("The reconciliation of man in Jesus Christ makes clear"), with the potential to overcome enmities ("The reconciliation of the world in Jesus Christ is the source"). If human beings embrace the project of reconciliation and start initiatives to challenge enmity by offering friendship to its victims, transformation may begin. Part of this process of reconciliation is to challenge sacrificial logics perpetuated by "economic imbalances, unjust social structures, exploitation of the defenseless, lack of knowledge" as very real forms of sociopolitical and economic structural enmity established and defended by legal systems.[21] This Social Creed as a creed of the church prefigures what the Methodist theologian Walter Wink has done in his very particular way fifteen years later.[22]

Responding to the same context as the Social Creed, liberation theologians such as Leonardo Boff also challenged sacrificial atonement theories and suggested replacing them with a narrative that interprets the cross as a symbol for an unconditional solidarity with humanity:

> As we have seen, the interpretation of the death of Christ as sacrifice is one of many. The New Testament texts themselves do not all allow the interpretation to be absolutized as it has been in the history of the faith within the Latin Church.

21 To me this is the essence of Ephesians 2:14–15 when it refers to the work of Christ as "having abolished in his flesh the enmity, *even* the law of commandments *contained* in ordinances" (emphasis added), at least when law is here not understood as restricted to religious laws but as a form to structure the Roman Empire.

22 See especially Walter Wink, *Violence and Nonviolence in South Africa* (Philadelphia: New Society, 1987), republished as *Jesus and Nonviolence: A Third Way* (Philadelphia: Augsburg Fortress, 2003); and Walter Wink, *When the Powers Fall: Reconciliation in the Healing of Nations* (Minneapolis: Fortress, 1998).

> Nevertheless, we ought to say that Christ's death was a consequence of the atmosphere of ill-will, hatred, and selfishness in which the Jews and all humanity lived and still live today. Jesus did not allow himself to be determined by this situation but loved us to the end. He took himself the perverted condition; he was in solidarity with us. He died alone so that no one else in the world would die alone; he is with each person so that all might partake of the life that manifested itself in the resurrection: eternal life in communion with God, with other/s, and with the cosmos.[23]

Obviously, with their 1971 Social Creed, Methodists addressed similar issues. This can be traced to the first change of the second article in 1888 and constantly from then on. In the late 1970s, the Brazilian Methodist Central Conference showed appreciation for parallel Catholic advances related to the theology of liberation, but they did not enter this dialogue with empty hands, and they were eager to communicate their theology to their people.[24] Coming back to the beginning of this chapter, Rauschenbusch's emphasis on solidarity and Bonhoeffer's understanding that the church can be the church (of Christ) only when it exists for others found their ways into the construction of a Brazilian Methodist identity. Its most famous expression is a motto coined in 1982: "Igreja Metodista, comunidade missionária ao serviço do povo" (Methodist Church, a missionary community in service to the people). However, as we shall see, this would not be the last word about the issue of how to describe best the relationship between the church and the world within the framework of reconciliation.

---

23 Leonardo Boff, *Jesus Christ Liberator: A Critical Christology for Our Time*, trans. Patrick Hughes (Maryknoll, NY: Orbis Books, 1978), 133.

24 See also Theodore W. Jennings Jr., *Transforming Atonement: A Political Theology of the Cross* (Minneapolis: Fortress, 2009), who shows the significance of one's preferential model of atonement.

A New Dimension: Reconciliation as Overcoming Human Enmity by Divine Friendship and Convivence

In the 1980s, the theology of atonement, which focused on overcoming human enmity by divine friendship, got a new format in Brazilian missiology, which applied it to the outer relations of the churches. Created as a Latin American contribution to mission encounters, the concept of *convivência* (convivence, in the sense of living together, side by side, or alongside one another) expressed a new approach.

Convivência was described first as the interaction between the Brazilian indigenous population and missional endeavors in the late 1970s and early 1980s. Soon thereafter, the German missiologist Theo Sundermeier introduced the concept to the European debate on "Ecumenical relations, European existence," and North-South relations; as a part of a xenology; and as a hermeneutic of encounter.[25] Sundermeier introduced the notion in German circles to counter Dietrich Bonhoeffer's idea of Christian existence as pro-existence, which he considered as too one-sided and not sufficiently cooperative or dialogical, and I think he made a good point.[26]

I cannot develop the whole discussion here in detail but would like to point out the strength of the concept of convivence, comparing it

25 Theo Sundermeier, "Konvivenz als Grundstruktur ökumenischer Existenz," *Ökumenische Existenz Heute* 1 (1986): 49–100; Theo Sundermeier, "Konvivenz: Ein Modell für Europa?" *International Journal of Orthodox Theology* 3 (2012): 4; Theo Sundermeier, "Sich verändern durch Zusammenleben. Konvivenz zwischen Nord und Süd," *Evangeische Kommentar* 89 (1986): 14–16; Theo Sundermeier, *Den Fremden wahrnehmen: Bausteine für eine Xenologie* (Gütersloh: Gütersloher Verlagshaus, 1992); Theo Sundermeier, *Den Fremden verstehen: Eine praktische Hermeneutik* (Göttingen: Vandenhoeck & Ruprecht, 1996).

26 Sundermeier, "Sich verändern durch Zusammenleben," 14. Since 1985, the British Methodist Church in Great Britain and Ireland talks about its "mission alongside the poor," and the Mission board of the United Methodist Church in Germany refers to its mission as "not a one-way street" ("Mission ist keine Einbahnstraße").

with other metaphors or concepts of the encounter of different people in one nation or between different nations. First, unlike the concept of the "melting pot," it does not pronounce unilateral self-negation or self-sacrifice, nor does it defend violent exclusion or apartheid; neither does it promote annexation or adaptation without guaranteeing specific rights for the integration of an incoming group. Last, but not least, it does not promote the potential unrelatedness of a mere multicultural proposal, which can produce ghettoization. *Convivência* makes sense not only for questions of ethnic and cultural identity but also for the challenge of creating open societies built on basic consensus and a commitment to invest in the common good by providing access to the mutual construction of the societies' political, social, economic, and ideological aspects.

I started to discuss the efficiency of the model in 1994 when I was responsible together with others for organizing an Afro-German Church in Hamburg, and I found it helpful to add another aspect: "convivence and cooperation."[27] Similarly, the Lutheran Brazilian theologian Rudolf von Sinner spoke of another essential ingredient in his work on "confidence and convivence."[28] Convivence needs faith and challenges it. Von Sinner grounded his proposal in two chapters on a Trinitarian argument.[29] In addition, I would suggest discussing convivence within the enmity-friendship framework or from a Christological and soteriological perspective. While I am not sure whether this

27 Helmut Renders, "So seid ihr nun nicht mehr Gäste und Fremdlinge, sondern Mitbürger der Heiligen und Gottes Hausgenossen: Erfahrungen und Gestaltung der Zusammenarbeit zwischen zwei Gemeinden ghanaischer und deutscher Prägung auf dem Bezirk Hamburg-Eppendorf der Evangelisch-methodistischen Kirche in Deutschland," DMin thesis, Wesley Theological Seminary, Washington, DC, 1998, esp. pp. 32–34.

28 Rudolf von Sinner, *Confiança e convivência: Reflexões éticas e ecumênicas* (São Leopoldo: Sinodal, 2007). Interestingly, Sinner refers only to Sundermeier and not to any Latin American authors.

29 To me the analogy between the immanent Trinity and the social life of human beings sounds idealistic, moralistic, and kind of overtaxing. I found a similar idea in Miroslav Volf, *Exclusion and Embrace: A Theological Exploration of Identity, Otherness and Reconciliation* (Nashville: Abingdon, 1996), 109.

ever has been done, I am convinced that to describe its theological legitimacy in soteriological and Christological terms and the theology of the cross would make for deeper roots, able to overcome the potential danger of its turning into the mere promotion of what Germans call "MultiKulti" (multi- or pluricultural societies) or, even worse, ghettoization. In his intriguing study *Exclusion and Embrace*, Miroslav Volf puts the problem of convivence challenged by wartime and conflicts the following way:

> "Too much injustice was done for us to be friends; too much blood was shed to live together," are the words that echo all too often in regions wrecked with conflict. A clear line will separate "them" from "us." They will remain "they" and we will remain "we," and we will never include "them" when we speak of "us." Such clean identities, living at safe distances from one another, may be all that is possible or even desirable in some cases at certain junctures of peoples' mutual history. But a parting of these ways is clearly not yet peace. Much more than just the absence of hostility sustained by the absence of contact, peace is *communion between former enemies.* Beyond offering forgiveness, Christ's passion aims at restoring such communion—even with the enemies that persistently refused to be reconciled.
>
> At the heart of the cross is Christ's stance of not letting the other remain an enemy and creating space within himself for the offender to come in. Read as the culmination of the larger narrative of God's dealing with humanity, the cross says that despite its manifest enmity towards God, humanity belongs to God; God will not be God without humanity.[30]

I would even say that the cross says that despite its manifest enmity toward God's humanity, "humanity"—now in a double sense—"belongs to God." Even without the inclusion of my alternative reading,

30 Volf, *Exclusion and Embrace*, 126.

Volf makes a strong claim, which to me translates what the Social Creed of the Methodist Church in Brazil said in 1971: the reconciliation of humanity in Jesus Christ indicates a way forward even in very hostile settings. Convivence is the attempt or endeavor to challenge enmities of all sorts by a new encounter, which interprets otherness as a gift and not as plague. Human diversity is like biodiversity: good, desirable, and helpful. In the Brazilian Methodist Church, this understanding of mission especially among the original population sustained the work of the missionary and later bishop Scilla Franco, who started his work in Mato Grosso do Sul alongside the Kaiowá and Terena in 1971.[31] The concept of convivence guided his work and entered an official document in 1999:

> **A Ministry as Convivence**
>
> The Methodist Church, from its pioneers John and Charles Wesley, has been called to learn from the Indians in dialogue and respect, and to serve them in humility and solidarity in the loving spirit of Jesus Christ and affirms their Christian responsibility for their integral well-being, expressed in the scriptures of the Old and New Testaments.
>
> Therefore, the Church understands that:
>
> A. Evangelization, as part of the Mission, is to incarnate divine love in the most diverse forms of human reality, so that Jesus Christ may be confessed as Lord, Savior, Deliverer **and Reconciler**. Evangelization signals and communicates the love of God in human life and in society through worship, proclamation, testimony, and service.

---

31 Scilla Franco, *Minha prece: Coletanea de textos indigenas e missionarios do Bispo Scilla Franco* (São Bernardo do Campo: EDITEO/Imprensa Metodista, 1992).

> B. The pastoral of coexistence presupposes being present with the indigenous community, participating in its daily life, learning, discovering and becoming a partner in the defense of life alongside the people. . . .
>
> C. The Gospel is only good news for indigenous peoples as it helps them to strengthen their own cultures to rebuild their rights on the land and to regain the dignity that the sons and daughters of God possess.[32]

The text contains a subtle nuance. By describing the role of evangelization as "to incarnate divine love . . . so that Jesus Christ may be confessed as Lord, Savior, Deliverer **and Reconciler,**" the church is confessing its own history of enmity toward indigenous populations and its necessity to be reconciled. It is evident here that the church is aware of its own potential for enmity as it goes into an intercultural encounter in a very privileged position. It represents an established institution that belongs to a very powerful, violent, and at the same time seductive society. Second, when the text describes "coexistence" as "participating . . . , learning, discovering and becoming a partner," reconciliation seems to be substituted or translated by reparation, but not in a classical theological sense, as in this case the dynamics of mutual sharing include not only the church offering Christ but also indigenous populations sharing their wisdom with the church as God's people. For sure, this articulation is more implicit than explicit, but it testifies to the revolutionary dynamics that the project of convivence still implied at the end of millennium. It still needs permanent actualization, however, as it has continued to be questioned by conservative missionary initiatives based on the classical sacrificial logic, which projects indigenous populations and their culture as enemies of God, and has

---

32 Methodist Church [in Brazil], *Book of Discipline* (Sao Paulo: Angular, 2016), 87.

effectively been challenged by an alliance between these groups and the current Brazilian government.[33]

A New Horizon: Reconciliation as Overcoming Human Enmity by Divine Friendship and Hospitality

The last concept I would like to connect with the enmity-friendship framework is the more recent appreciation of the praxis of hospitality. Again, I suggest doing this within the framework of its New Testament connotations, referring to "fellow-citizens with the saints, and of the household of God" and a specific economy of salvation.[34]

As far as I can see it at the moment, this discussion is developed mainly in the third world, often in response to migration. In the Methodist Church in Brazil, it has not arrived at an institutional level. In other places, it is promoted by philosophers, with a wide response among theologians, especially practical or pastoral ones.[35] The positions clos-

33 Helmut Renders, "Convivência: coragem de uma missão sensível e profética," *Expositor Cristão* (São Paulo), January 15, 2002, 3. At the beginning of the new millennium, new mission concepts emerged. See Helmut Renders, "Entre 'Tupi ou não Tupi' ou a (não tão) ingênua continuação da conquista? Elementos para um referencial teórico de uma teologia amazônida metodista," *Caminhando* 8, no. 2 (2003): 212–22; and Helmut Renders, "A Igreja Metodista na Amazônia e a Questão da Amazônia," in *Meio Ambiente e Missão*: A responsabilidade ecológica das igrejas, ed. Clovis Pinto de Castro (São Bernardo do Campo, SP: EDITEO, 2003), 135–54.

34 Ephesians 2:19. The description of the partaking in the household as fellow-citizens seems to include a more egalitarian understanding of its relations, again a quite revolutionary aspect considering Roman households. In our time, this idea still challenges forms of patronizing relationships.

35 Jacques Derrida and Anne Dufourmsantelle, *Of Hospitality*, trans. Rachel Bowlby (Stanford, CA: Stanford University Press, 2000); Arthur Sutherland, *I Was a Stranger: A Christian Theology of Hospitality* (Nashville: Abingdon, 2006); Pamela J. Buck and Christine Pohl, *Making Room: Recovering Hospitality as a Christian Tradition* (Grand Rapids, MI: Eerdmans, 2001); Daniel

est to mine are surely feminist and postcolonial perspectives.[36] This is because they remember the radical roots of hospitality, preserved in the Greek word *philoxenia*, the brotherly and sisterly love for the stranger, the strange, the different other. *Philoxenia* is the opposite of xenophobia, homophobia, and all the other forms of rejection and exclusion. For sure, the stranger is not necessarily an enemy. This becomes clearer when we study the Bible. In biblical Hebrew, the authors use three different words not only to name but also to describe strangers: *zar*, *nacre,* and *gar*. *Zar* represents the rich political or military enemy; *nacre* is a person who may be a residing salesperson, who is respected but not integrated into the community; *gar* is a poor stranger who came to Israel, for example, as an immigrant or a refugee. They—and only they—are considered strangers worthy of care from the faith community, alongside widows and orphans.

In the New Testament, these privileges of a *gar* are extended by God in Christ to all humankind. Whereas, in general, hospitality refers in Greek to a *xenos*, a stranger, Ephesians 2:11–19 demonstrates that both concepts, stranger and enemy whose enmity has to be overcome, were seen in approximation to one another. The text parallels "the cross, having slain the enmity thereby" (Eph. 2:16), with "no more strangers and foreigners, but fellow-citizens" (Eph. 2:19).[37] The discussion about hospitality belongs to the later texts of the New Testament,

---

Homan and Lonni Collins Pratt, *Radical Hospitality: Benedict's Way of Love*, 2nd ed. (Brewster, MA: Paraclete, 2005).

36 Letty Mandeville Russell, "Postcolonial Challenges and the Practice of Hospitality," in *A Just and True Love: Feminism and the Frontiers of Theological Ethics: Essays in Honor of Margaret A. Farley*, ed. Maura Ryan and Brian Linnane (Notre Dame, IN: University of Notre Dame Press, 2007), 109–33; Letty Mandeville Russell, *Just Hospitality: God's Welcome in a World of Difference* (Louisville, KY: Westminster John Knox, 2009).

37 Therefore, Ephesians makes a point that may lead us to attribute to the migrant and stranger the right not only of visitation but also of residence, to understand sanctuary churches and cities not as the end but a means to the concept that no one is illegal. See Thomas Nail, "Migrant Cosmopolitanism," *Public Affairs Quarterly* 29, no. 2 (2015): 187–99.

and the affirmation in Hebrews that *xenoi* can be angels (Hebrew 13:2) is probably one of the most beautiful and poetic forms to describe otherness as potentially divine. Moreover, the first virtue of a bishop, following Titus, is the promotion of *philoxenia* (Tit. 1:8). Hospitality, as *philoxenia*, which proposes to overcome different levels of enmity or the traumatic remembrance of vulnerability and displacement as a stranger by friendship, finds its deepest roots in the soteriological dimension of the theology of reconciliation and its aim to overcome enmity by nothing else but friendship.

Returning to Brazilian Methodism, which in the last twenty years has invested a lot of energy in discipleship programs, I believe it would be revolutionary to combine these efforts with its long-term focus on reconciliation as overcoming human enmity by divine friendship, or in the terms of Bonhoeffer, with focus on discipleship as grounding friends and members of the Church in the message of reconciliation by practicing the overcoming of enmity by friendship.

Final Considerations

I hope that I was able to clarify why I consider the ministry of reconciliation as "deep" revolution in potential, in reference, and with appreciation for the theological and ecclesiastical work being done by an independent Methodist Church still associated with Methodism. I see a constant will and ability to challenge frontiers, learn within cultural and social boundaries, and explore possibilities, nurtured by a theology of reconciliation as the *cantus firmus.* I believe that this exploration was revolutionary, and that the change of the second article of the Articles of Religion, the Social Creed of 1971 concerning the public witness of the church, and the application of convivence deserve our respect.

I am also convinced that the paradigm of hospitality should be integrated into the discipleship program. This would be a distinct contribution of Brazilian Methodism to the people and to Brazilian society. It has to address enmity and create spaces with the potential to overcome it. The theology of reconciliation is a consistent way to accomplish these goals, and the concepts of hospitality and convivence are its inner and outer practice and practical expression. Challenging the boundaries of enmity by offering friendship may help the churches to grow in their ecumenical and social commitment in times when fear of violence and enmity, whether from governments or social movements, as well as fear of loss of power and privileges, seems to overrun them.

In the nineteenth century Methodists wanted to be known as "friends of all and enemies of none." This never was meant as an invitation to avoid positions, not to take sides, not to commit oneself, but it should be understood as a soteriological statement: be not the cause of enmity, but if there is enmity, overcome it by nothing else but perseverant friendship.[38] That is the way God has overcome enmity in Jesus Christ and keeps overcoming it in the Church and in the world.

---

38 Here is not the time and place to develop this idea further, but I interpret "perseverant friendship" as nonviolent resistance based on a firm theology of convivence and hospitality. I greatly appreciate the work done by Mennonite theologians on this topic. The key reference for my own work is the Methodist theologian Walter Wink.

PART TWO

Contemporary Challenges

CHAPTER THREE

Queering Wesley, Queering the Church

Toward an Ecclesial Circumcision of the Heart

KEEGAN OSINSKI

Keywords: queer, queering, queer reading, circumcision, holiness, church

Introduction

Wesleyan Holiness churches find their name and identity in their understanding and practice of *holiness*, that is, a certain flavor of Christian living in which the ultimate focus and goal is the perfect love of God and neighbor as exemplified in the life of Jesus Christ and empowered by the work of the Holy Spirit. In so doing, these churches may often look to the margins, where Jesus would be most likely to dwell—with the poor, the sick, the outcast. John Wesley himself emphasized the importance of being in community and solidarity with the marginalized, not only to help them in their need but also to engage with and learn from them as the locus of God's presence in the world.

This chapter will offer a queer reading of Wesley's 1733 sermon "The Circumcision of the Heart," in an effort to show that the perspectives of LGBTQ+[1] people have vital contributions to make within the holiness traditions that so often marginalize them. Reading Wesley queerly offers unique insights for thinking of holiness—the core aspect of our faith—as an expansive openness to the grace of God rather than a limiting and restrictive legalism. Indeed, such a reading will not be "a setter forth of new doctrines" but will preach only, as Wesley did, "Jesus and the resurrection."[2] That which may sound queer to our ears will reflect only "the most essential duties of Christianity":[3] to love God with one's whole heart and to love one's neighbor as oneself.

The chapter will consist of three parts: first, an analysis of the queerness of the concept "circumcision of the heart," as presented in Wesley's sermon and in scripture; second, a reading of holiness as queer, which, in addition to engaging Wesley's sermon, will engage the work of queer theologians and theorists; and third, some consequences and implications for the life and practice of Wesleyan Holiness churches in light of the queerness of circumcision-of-the-heart holiness.

Contextual Considerations

At the outset, in the interest of clarity, let me offer definitions of *queer, queering,* and *queer reading.* I use *queer* as an adjective to signify that

---

1 There are many renderings of this abbreviation, the most common being LGBT, which serves to identify the community of lesbian, gay, bisexual, and transgender people. I choose to expand it with the addition of the letter Q, signifying queer, which may have numerous additional significations, for gender and sexuality, biology, and politics. I also choose to include the "+" to signify the panoply of other discrete identities, such as intersex and asexual, which deserve recognition but would be impossible to list upon each mention.

2 John Wesley, "The Circumcision of the Heart," in *The Works of John Wesley,* vol. 1, ed. Albert L. Outler (Nashville: Abingdon, 1984), 401. All references to the sermon will be to this edition.

3 Wesley, "Circumcision of the Heart," 401.

which is not normative, particularly as relating to sex, gender, sexuality, and the expressions thereof. I will use *queer* as a verb to mean engaging in the practice of problematizing normative narratives and assumptions—those givens that perpetuate power structures that baptize and uphold some norms while damning and marginalizing alternative ways of being. Methodist scholar Pamela Lightsey says that "queering, as a theological methodology, is a deconstruction and re-evaluation of gender perspectives that uses as its framework queer theory and as its resources scripture, reason, tradition, and experience."[4] She evokes a queered version of the so-called Wesleyan Quadrilateral—the well-loved and oft-cited framework for evaluating authority within Wesleyan traditions—that centers the queer reading of scripture and the reason, tradition, and experience of queer people. And finally, I define a queer reading as an attempt to queer—that is, disrupt and interrogate the sex, gender, and sexuality norms of—a given text. To read queerly is to look at a text from different angles and through different eyes, to see what's missing or what takes up too much space, to explore all the possibilities of what the text could be saying, and to tease out what might be hiding closeted within the text.

Queering Circumcision

To be circumcised in the first place is, in some way, to be made queer. It is to alter a sexual organ to something other than "natural" and, further, to subscribe to a mode of being that is supernatural. It is an anti-normative act following an anti-normative code.

In the Hebrew Bible, circumcision is first introduced in Genesis 17. God says to Abraham, "This is my covenant, which you shall keep, between me and you and your offspring after you: Every male among you shall be circumcised."[5] The cutting of the foreskin of the males of Abraham's family was to be a sign of his covenant with God,

---

4 Pamela Lightsey, *Our Lives Matter* (Eugene, OR: Pickwick, 2015), 27.

5 Genesis 17:10. All biblical text in this chapter will be from the NRSV.

which promised that Abraham would be "the ancestor of a multitude of nations" (Gen. 17:4). If any male of this multitude of offspring (or any male brought into the family by purchase or other means) did not have his foreskin cut off, he would be cut off from the family and therefore from God. Therefore, in demanding the practice of circumcision, God was creating a queer community, marked by the difference of their genitals as belonging to each other and to God.

Joshua 4 says that Joshua had to circumcise all the male Israelites before they entered the Promised Land. All the circumcised Israelites who had left from Egypt had died in the forty intervening years, and the children born in the wilderness "had not been circumcised on the way" (Josh. 4:7), and so before this peculiar people could enter their own land, they had to be circumcised to remind them of their queerness as the people of God who were receiving their promise. This material queerness was essential in constructing the Israelites' identity as the people of God.

Historically, circumcision has been a point of departure for anti-Semitism, deeply intertwined with misogyny. Daniel Boyarin explains that "the (male) Jewish body has been feminized: male Jews menstruate in the folklore of much of Europe, and circumcision has been repeatedly blamed for the femaleness (weakness, passivity) of the Jew."[6] The transgender queerness of the menstruating circumcised male served as one justification for the oppression of all Jews, simultaneously putting down people who were circumcised and people who menstruated as weak and nonnormative, that is, not identifying with the ideal strong, white Christian European man. This combination of stigma, placed on Jews by the dominant group, reminds us that the word *queer* itself is and has been used as a slur and is only now being reclaimed in constructive moves of theory and community.[7] That which falls outside the hegemonic norms is denigrated and ridiculed into submission or

6 Daniel Boyarin, *A Radical Jew* (Oakland: University of California Press, 1997), 17.

7 Patrick Cheng explains that "the LGBT community has taken a word that was originally viewed as a highly offensive slur and transformed it into a positive

extinction.[8] For Jews to hold on to circumcision—this queer mark—in the face of threat, harm, and ridicule is to assert a radical allegiance to a queer identity that is ultimately the specific grace and gifting of God. It is to embrace this God-given identity and follow God in God's promise to God's people rather than submit to the powers that would have the Jewish people conform to worldly norms.

To circumcise the *heart*, then, is to further queer the practice. In the circumcision of the heart, circumcision becomes no longer restricted to and by gender and sex but rather is made open to (or indeed required of) all who would follow God. The first instance of the circumcision of the heart in the Hebrew Bible is in Deuteronomy 10:14–18:

> Although heaven and the heaven of heavens belong to the Lord your God, the earth with all that is in it, yet the Lord set his heart in love on your ancestors alone and chose you, their descendants after them, out of all the peoples, as it is today. Circumcise, then, the foreskin of your heart, and do not be stubborn any longer. For the Lord your God is God of gods and Lord of lords, the great God, mighty and awesome, who is not partial and takes no bribe, who executes justice for the orphan and the widow, and who loves the strangers, providing them food and clothing.

The passage talks about God's requirements of God's people, including fearing, serving, and loving God as well as caring for the stranger. None of these acts of devotion, of course, is restricted by genital configuration, much less gender expression or sexual orientation. Loving God and loving others is the universal call for *all* of God's people, and this seems to be the result of a circumcised heart.

---

description of the incredible diversity and transgressivity that is within the community." *From Sin to Amazing Grace* (New York: Seabury, 2012), xvii.

8 Some extreme examples are the Shoah or the 1998 murder of Matthew Shepard in Wyoming.

In Jeremiah 4:4, the prophet says:

Circumcise yourselves to the LORD,
remove the foreskin of your hearts,
O people of Judah and inhabitants of Jerusalem,
or else my wrath will go forth like fire,
and burn with no one to quench it,
because of the evil of your doings.

Here it seems that to circumcise, or remove the foreskin of, one's heart is the opposite of, or the antidote to, "evil in your doings." The circumcision of the heart is what keeps God's people from God's wrath.

Further, while genital circumcision was a point of contention in early Christianity, whether followers of Jesus should be circumcised as Jews or not,[9] the spiritual, rather than material, "circumcision of the heart" is taken up as the mark of the Christian. Indeed, in the text Wesley focuses on in this sermon, Paul asserts against the Judaizers that "*real* circumcision is a matter of the heart" (Rom. 2:29; emphasis added) and that the literal circumcision of the penis is actually inconsequential in the eyes of God. What God *really* cares about is not the state of one's genitals but the state of one's heart. Whereas literal circumcision requires a penis—and specifically a biologically "normative" one at that—the metaphorical circumcision of the heart is not limited to a certain genital configuration.

To circumcise the heart is similarly to be made queer in that, like genital circumcision, it is a resistance to normative powers and expectations.[10] Wesley says that "the circumcision of the heart, the seal of thy calling, is foolishness with the world,"[11] that is, it is *queer*. It is contrary to the world's normative expectations of how a life should be lived. Where one might be expected to be self-preserving and thrifty,

9 See Paul's letters, especially those to the Galatians and the Corinthians.

10 It is worth noting, if just briefly to bring up the question, that circumcision actually *is* the norm in the United States and has been for some time. What does it mean when the nonnormative or nonnatural becomes the norm?

11 Wesley, "Circumcision of the Heart," 402.

God calls for God's people to provide for the poor and the widow and care for complete strangers. This selfless behavior is certainly contrary to the norms of the world—particularly the twenty-first-century Western capitalist world—that prizes individual success and wealth above all else, even sometimes contrary to personal desires for security and power. Just as the Jews' embrace of their circumcision is an embrace of a certain queerness, to embrace the circumcision of the heart that Wesley pulls from scripture is to embrace a certain queerness. That queer, self-giving, justice-seeking life that Christians are called to, for which we are marked by our hearts' circumcision, is the life of holiness.

Queering Holiness

I have established that we might characterize circumcision of the heart as queer. Additionally, Wesley asserts that circumcision of the heart is characterized as holiness. Therefore, perhaps holiness may also be considered queer.

Wesley's sermon consists of two parts: first, the question of the nature of the circumcision of the heart and, second, some reflections on that nature. He concludes, in the first place, that circumcision of the heart, in general, is *holiness*, that is, the "habitual disposition of the soul . . . which implies being cleansed from sin . . . and endued with those virtues which were also in Christ Jesus."[12] This disposition and these virtues are exhibited, as Wesley says, not by any outward form but by "a right state of soul, a mind and spirit renewed after the image of Him that created it."[13] In a queer paradigm, gender or sexuality may not be deduced simply by an outward form such as genital configuration, and similarly, for Wesley, holiness requires an examination of the state of the *heart*. While one may think it easy to deduce by another's outward form whether they've been cleansed from sin or whether their spirit has

12 Ibid., 402–3.

13 Ibid., 402.

been renewed to be like Christ's, Wesley here insists to the contrary that holiness is a matter of the heart.

In particular, Wesley uses the second part of his sermon to assert that holiness has four markers: humility, faith, hope, and charity. These four markers might be surprising if one were to expect holiness to be marked by, or entirely consist of, other characteristics of piety and purity, like submission, preservation, decency, or control. But these are not the markers Wesley sees or emphasizes. The markers of holiness that Wesley identifies are not in the static, austere, preservationist paradigm of holiness that fears contamination but rather are markers of a queer paradigm of openness to all kind of nonnormative difference that transforms lives into queer Christlikeness.

Humility, faith, hope, and love can be markers of queerness as well as holiness, rendering Wesley's presentation of holiness as queer. Looking at how these markers of holiness find their expression in the lives and thought of LGBTQ+ Christians and theorists can help us problematize and reconstruct the ideas of humility, faith, hope, and love as they are presented in a restrictive heteronormative paradigm and expand how we understand them and what they might look like in practice. Let us now consider each of these markers and how they might be read as queer, thereby queering holiness itself.

Humility

Humility, at the first, is for Wesley "a right judgment of ourselves," particularly regarding "the sinfulness and helplessness of our nature."[14] For queer people, being told they are sinful and helpless is nothing new. Indeed, they have *been humbled* by Church and society. In the normative hierarchy of cisheteropatriarchy—that is, the structure of society in which cisgendered, heterosexual men establish and maintain norms—the queer are firmly placed in the slots at the bottom, the slots of humility. In fact, we might say that in being humbled, queer people have actually had a *wrong* judgment of themselves imparted upon them.

14 Ibid., 403.

Feminist theologian Valerie Saiving Goldstein suggests in her classic essay "The Human Situation: A Feminine View" that the entire conception of sin in Western Christianity has been centered on male (and, we could add, heterosexual) experience, and in particular the experience of pride, which is why pride is considered to be at the core of sin.[15] She says that this male conception of sin is essentially pride in that it is characterized by "magnifying its own power, righteousness, or knowledge" and that "sin is the unjustified concern of the self for its own power and prestige."[16] However, Saiving Goldstein asserts, this male experience and conception of sin as pride is not the same as the feminine experience of sin. Further, she argues, if sin is something experienced by all people, its conception should be characterized by a common experience, not by the (straight, cisgendered) male experience, which is different from the female (or homosexual, or transgender, etc.) experience.

The issue of pride and humility as the loci of sin and holiness, respectively, is then problematized—for men and women, and people of other genders, as well as for people of various sexualities. If pride is not in fact an essential characteristic of sin in all people, we must rethink what role humility plays in a universalized conception of holiness. Saiving Goldstein's argument can be expanded from being primarily about women to the LGBTQ+ community as well. Just as pride is not the essential characteristic of feminine sin, according to Saiving Goldstein, perhaps neither is it the essential characteristic of LGBTQ+ sin. Patrick Cheng quotes Elizabeth Stuart's suggestion that "the 'sin' of LGBT people is not so much 'individual disobedience rooted in pride,' but rather 'not loving ourselves enough, of not having enough pride in ourselves.' "[17] Instead of the straight, cisgendered male sin of pride that must be remedied with holy humility, the LGBTQ+ conception of sin

15 See Augustine, *City of God,* book 14, sections 13–14.

16 Valerie Saiving Goldstein, "The Human Situation: A Feminine View," in *Readings in Ecology and Feminist Theology,* ed. Mary Heather MacKinnon and Moni McIntyre (New York: Sheed and Ward, 1995), 4.

17 Cheng, *From Sin to Amazing Grace,* 114.

might be a different kind of wrong judgment of self, which must be remedied by a kind of holy pride. If, as Wesley says, humility is having a right judgment of oneself, for queer folk "humility," in the holiness sense, may actually look a lot like "pride."[18] Wesleyan churches may indeed have committed the sin of pride in judging themselves as better, more right, or more holy than LGBTQ+ people. To right this wrong may indeed require the embrace of a queer holiness in which all people may judge themselves rightly as beloved creations of God struggling together for redemption and justice.

Faith

Wesley says that "the best guide of the blind . . . is faith."[19] It is telling that the best guide of the blind is not *sight* or *light* but *faith*. Holiness does not require us to be shaped into exemplars of normative wholeness determined by a hegemonic definition of what is right and good but rather to yield to the guidance and provision of God, embracing our bodies, abilities, and identities in light of that faith. Resisting the demand for bodies to conform to this hegemonic ideal is queer. And here, we see, it is also faithful.

Indeed, attaining this kind of singular ideal of wholeness and holiness in terms of gender and sexuality is impossible. For instance, in her book *Sex/Gender: Biology in a Social World*, Anne Fausto-Sterling says that "there are probably so many contributing streams [in the development of human embryos] and they probably interact in so many different ways, that we will never have a single story to tell about gender development."[20] The very development of humans and their genders and sexualities is queer. The complex contingencies of development resist norms at every turn. The faith of a queer holiness does not trust

---

18 Elizabeth Edman argues exactly this in her book *Queer Virtue: What LGBTQ People Know about Life and Love and How It Can Revitalize Christianity* (Boston: Beacon, 2016), which I will discuss in the next section.

19 Wesley, "Circumcision of the Heart," 404.

20 Anne Fausto-Sterling, *Sex/Gender: Biology in a Social World* (New York: Routledge, 2012), 57.

in a God who transforms people by a Stepford-like mold into models of perfect submission and docility, of heterosexuality and straight gender. Rather, the faith of queer holiness trusts in a God who creates in an infinite diversity, the Leviathan frolicking in the *tehom,* and calls all God's creation *tov.* The chaotic abyss of the deep produces a creation that is good, acceptable, perfect, and whole in all its abundant anarchic variety.

In faith, there is risk—risk of difference and conflict and untamable passion—but risk is what makes faith real. Faith founded in certainty, sameness, and safety is no faith at all. Ethicist Mark Jordan identifies this un-faith of certainty as the "vice of the obligatory answer"—the assumption that there must be a rule for every question Christian ethics must answer.[21] A so-called faith that champions and shelters norms and ideals rather than chasing after risk and encouraging creativity and exploration is beholden to this vice, not to the God witnessed to by the faith of queer holiness.

In fact, the vice of the obligatory answer values right-knowing so much that it covers over and smooths out any ambiguity or unevenness in tradition, scripture, experience, or reason in order to create and subsequently adhere to a norm. For example, Jordan points out that the words *sodomy* and *homosexuality* are not found in the Bible (though some translators have rendered words as such), and that other words such as *fornication* and *adultery* actually conceal as much as they reveal.[22] To pretend to know all meanings and applications of scripture while ignoring its complexity and ambiguity, and further to do so in a way that harms and marginalizes others, cannot be the work of holiness faith. A queer faith that is the surest guide of the blind is a faith

21 Mark Jordan, *Ethics of Sex* (Hoboken, NJ: Wily-Blackwell, 2002), 7.

22 Ibid., 23. Jordan goes on to point out that churches tend to cite the Bible as if it is a coherent, universal code. Besides the fact that it is not coherent or universal, most of the sexual prohibitions they point to in Leviticus, to condemn homosexuality, for instance, are "part of a system of purity taboos that Christians have not observed." So to use the Bible in this prescriptive way is rather nonsensical.

that trusts not in the certainty and sureness of light or sight but in the risk-taking, creative, and all-loving God, the author of the gloriously uncertain, ambiguous, and queer creation.

Nazarene theologian Mildred Bangs Wynkoop says that "faith is not the boundary around the Christian which sets him apart and defines him. It is the 'growing edge' which keeps him from mere definition and makes him a flowing-out life, a dynamo of love."[23] Faith is not defining, then, in the sense that it makes the life of the Christian *definite*, but instead it is the point of departure from where Christians might fling ourselves into the risk of life and love. Faith is the openness to the *infinite*. Faith is a transformative trust in all the various and mysterious actions of God. Therefore, inasmuch as this wide-open faith of holiness leads us in our blindness along a path toward loving God-knows-what, there is a very good chance that this faith is queer.

Hope

For Wesley, hope is the assurance of the Spirit that a person is indeed "in the path which leadeth to life," aided by God to persevere.[24] This hope and perseverance requires discipline, that is, "daily care" to rid the heart of pollution. The pollution Wesley describes includes uncleanness, envy, malice, and wrath, passions and tempers that are "after the flesh."[25] Like humility, hope requires a right judgment of ourselves and our sin—an identification that it is couched in, and must be cut out of, the heart.

Sin, according to Wesley's sermon, is located in "passions and tempers"—in other words, dispositions—thereby, opposite to such sin stands hope as an assurance of God's provision and help to do the work of purifying the heart. This is not a kind of spiritual calorie counting to stay on the right track; rather, holiness hopes in God to will our

23 Mildred Bangs Wynkoop, *A Theology of Love* (Kansas City: Beacon Hill, 1972), 248.

24 Wesley, "Circumcision of the Heart," 406.

25 Ibid., 407.

purification against calculation. This becomes more telling when one notices that much of Wesley's discussion of discipline takes place in his discussion of hope.

For example, Wesley believes discipline must be intimately tied to hope, signaling that the discipline he believes is required for holiness is not based in a kind of will to power (which would be part of the sin of pride) but rather is based in the hope that God will do it, that God *is* doing it, that God's prevenient grace goes ahead of us and makes our way for holiness. Holiness hopes in God that the dispositions of our heart will ultimately be rooted not in evil but in love—perhaps any and all kinds of love that move us away from envy, malice, wrath, and uncleanness. Further, in a heteronormative paradigm, "uncleanness" may immediately signal some kind of (perhaps homo-)sexual impropriety, but when thinking queerly, we may notice that its parallelism with envy, malice, and wrath—again, dispositions of the heart—makes it out to be perhaps something more like an unlovely way of thinking or a desire driven by selfishness or greed. For all the airtime given to the Christian obsession with sexual sins, in Christians' use of the Bible and the tradition of the church, sexual sins have only been one aspect—indeed a small one—of what is considered sin.

Thinking of LGBTQ+ issues specifically, Patrick Cheng points out that of more than thirty-one thousand verses in the Bible, the church has focused in on just six to construct its beliefs about homosexuality.[26] Therefore to assume "uncleanness" would refer solely or primarily to sexual sin—and homosexuality, at that—is grossly misguided. The hope of holiness is in a broader, more holistic wholeness that brings the whole person into perfect love, in all aspects of life, not hung up on genital acts alone. And further, because of Wesley's, and his reading of the Bible's, emphasis on the state of the heart as the progenitor of sin or love, we might conclude that holiness is not about the genital acts at all but rather the intent behind and consequences subsequent to those acts. Certainly some queer sex or relationships might be sinful,

26 Cheng, *From Sin to Amazing Grace,* 17.

unclean, unlovely, driven by selfishness or greed, just as some heterosexual sex or relationships might be. But, as Wendy Farley points out, "there is no call for heterosexual men to deny their sexuality altogether because some of them use it badly."[27] The persevering discipline in hope that Wesley is calling for in this sermon is a discipline toward a holistic holiness that is centered on love—inclusive of the whole person and their acts and, primarily, dispositions, that they would be characterized by love rather than evil.

We might also question what "uncleanness" and "cleanness" really are in the first place and how conventional distinctions become muddied in the life of Jesus, who ate with sinners and prostitutes, or in the stories of Jesus, like the ritually "clean" Levite leaving the injured man in the ditch while the "unclean" Samaritan helps him. Perhaps the circumcision of the heart is not as clean a cut as we might think.

Later in the sermon, Wesley briefly identifies hope with joy.[28] The assurance granted by hope frees people from the fear of risk, if not the uncertainty. It liberates people to take the risk of faith with abandon. There is certainly little structure or regimen or will to power in outright joy. One of the most common biblical examples of joy is in 2 Samuel 6, where David dances before the Lord, shamelessly uncovering himself—very queer indeed.

Charity

Finally, Wesley adds as the crowning marker of the circumcision of the heart charity, or love. Love, he says, "is all the commandments in one," and in love, ultimately, is perfection and holiness. He, of course, cites what he calls the "royal law of heaven and earth"—"Thou shalt love the Lord thy God with all thy heart, and with all thy soul, and with all thy mind, and with all thy strength"—but he is quick to point out that (a) this does not forbid us to love anything other than God, and in fact

27 Wendy Farley, *Gathering Those Driven Away* (Louisville, KY: Westminster John Knox, 2011), 3.

28 Wesley, "Circumcision of the Heart," 411.

it implies that we *do* love others; and (b) it does not forbid us to take pleasure in anything other than God.[29] Therefore it is clear for Wesley that any true, unselfish love and pleasure that points to God is wrapped up in holiness. Indeed, this is a radical affirmation of all love and pleasure, perhaps even queer love and pleasure, inasmuch as it leads to God. Christine Gudorf argues that pleasure is itself a "premoral good," that is, though it does not necessarily lead to moral good, it is "ordinarily a good, and should be understood as one aspect of the general social good."[30] She discusses mutual sexual pleasure, especially, as a stage where we act out the injunction to love our neighbor as ourselves. She says that Christians often assume that loving the neighbor entails a denial of self; however, "sex is perhaps one of the best life arenas for demonstrating that self and other are not naturally hostile" and that "the interests of the self and the interests of the partner are largely linked."[31] Therefore, in the engagement of sexual pleasure, we very clearly love our neighbor as we love ourselves, thereby obeying God's law and demonstrating our love of God as well. In this way, any mutual sexual pleasure rooted in love can be a vital part of holiness. If love is the clearest and most important indicator of holiness, then surely we would do well to read "love" as inclusive of all the various kinds of love found in all the various kinds of relationship experienced between people—romantic and sexual, even gay, lesbian, bisexual, pansexual, or polyamorous, and also platonic, parental, filial, asexual, erotic, temporary, enduring, and existing in the multitude of contours and expressions we see in our world. To limit what counts as love would be to put a limit on holiness, even the holiness of God, who has no limits.

Queering the Church

If circumcision of the heart is marked by humility, faith, hope, and charity, how might we think about such circumcision ecclesially? What

---

29 Ibid., 407–8.

30 Christine Gudorf, *Body, Sex, and Pleasure* (Cleveland: Pilgrim, 1994), 90.

31 Ibid., 94.

does such a queer circumcision marked by a queered understanding of humility, faith, hope, and love look like in the church?

Perhaps the church might be circumcised by humility, such that we acknowledge that our place is not the seat of judgment whence we might demand adherence to some standard morality and behavior of questionable provenance. If the queer are already the humble, by virtue of their marginalization, perhaps the call for humility in the call for holiness is directed at the heteronormative status quo of the church, in which we need to identify our own "corrupt nature," that "confusion and ignorance and error reign over our understanding," and that perhaps the church itself needs to cleanse its mind "from those high conceits of our own perfection,"[32] acknowledging that the grace and love of God, not a heteropatriarchal hierarchy, should be the chief dictate of our behavior and relationships. Indeed, the church might learn from those queer people it has marginalized how to have a "right judgment of ourselves," that is, not only to identify and acknowledge our propensity for sin and infirmity but also to embrace the inalienable *imago dei* in ourselves with all others. In Elizabeth Edman's book *Queer Virtue*, she identifies queer pride as one of the virtues embodied by the LGBTQ+ community that the church would do well to emulate. She asserts that "pride begins first and foremost with the ability to see oneself."[33] In other words, we might say that pride is "a right judgment of ourselves," which is exactly how Wesley defines humility. A reversal of pride and humility may be in order to achieve a queer holiness in a queer church. Edman goes on to say that "defining sin as pride, as hubris, may be appropriate for people of privilege . . . but for those who have been colonized, dehumanized, demonized" it can "extend and exacerbate oppression."[34] Such a reversal is entirely consistent with, indeed emblematic of, the kingdom of God, in which the exalted are humbled and the humbled exalted. Therefore, the least our churches

32 Wesley, "Circumcision of the Heart," 403.

33 Edman, *Queer Virtue*, 109.

34 Ibid., 115.

can do is include our queer friends, the least among us, in our congregations and our leadership.

Perhaps the church might be circumcised by faith, such that we come to rely not on our own sight, following the path we see as right in our own eyes, but rather on the provision of the gracious God, who leads us in the way of righteousness and love. To inhabit spaces of normative privilege (to be, for the sake of the metaphor, "sighted") is, indeed, only to see in part. The eyes of faith are those that "pull down strongholds," "overturn all prejudices of corrupt reason," and "cast down every high thing that exalteth itself against the knowledge of God."[35] The eyes of faith are not the eyes of the normative powers; they are the queer eyes that see as Christ sees. To look on others with the queer eyes of faith is to look toward mutual liberation. It is to disrupt the systems that exclude and reject and place themselves as the ultimate authority and rule rather than God. The eyes of faith direct our touching, tasting queer blindness toward God's love, which does not restore our sight but transforms it.

A church marked by queer faith embraces people as they are, trusting that the God who made them, who loves them, is faithful to work in them as God will. A church marked by queer faith embodies the belief of church mothers cooing over the newest tiny congregant, that "God don't make no junk." God knows what God is doing, even when what God is doing seems queer beyond our reckoning. A church marked by queer faith takes all the risks required by a true hospitality to the other, a true love and acceptance of the neighbor and the stranger alike.

Perhaps the church might be circumcised by hope, in which we have joyful assurance of God doing God's work in all hearts to rid them of evil and fill them with love. This hope manifests as joy in the divine fulfillment of holiness in us, not as anxiety rooted in achieving some purity of our own design and effort. So perhaps this hope looks like denying the impulse to require adherence to a strict code of conduct but rather abiding in the queer hope that God works in hearts

35 Wesley, "Circumcision of the Heart," 404–5.

in an abundant diversity of ways, all leading toward Christian perfection, freedom, and holiness. A denial of legalism and dependence on codes frees us to take responsibility for our own spiritual discipline. It requires us to practice conforming our lives to the perfect love of God and neighbor and to wrestle with what that means in our lives individually and ecclesially. The discipline of learning to love is messy when there are no facile rules to fall back on, yet we have hope that God is in that mess with us, guiding us in and toward the love God has commanded of us. In the discipline of queer hope there is no striving but rest. Rather than looking for some future glory, for some unattainable perfection in the distance, queer hope brings that glory into the present and says that perfection of love can be ours now—a thoroughly Wesleyan teaching. As we sing in the Fanny Crosby hymn "Blessed Assurance":

> Perfect submission, perfect delight!
> Visions of rapture now burst on my sight;
> Angels descending bring from above
> Echoes of mercy, whispers of love.[36]

A church marked by queer hope leans into the joyful assurance that God is working now to transform our hearts from progenitors of evil dispositions to founts of perfect love, and that the discipline this requires is not about acting "good" or morally respectable so that we may receive mercy and love in the future but hoping in and receiving the work God is doing in all people here and now.

And perhaps the church might be circumcised by love, wherein the love and affection toward others—particularly marginalized others—as well as all manner of pleasure might contribute to and bolster our holiness, inasmuch as it leads us to love the one who is the creator of such love and pleasure. That is, rather than hide from, reject, or proscribe queer varieties of love, the church might embrace them as equal

---

36 Fanny J. Crosby, "Blessed Assurance," in *The United Methodist Hymnal* (Nashville: United Methodist Publishing House, 1989), 369.

and valid conduits of loving God. Holiness churches have been afraid of pleasure for too long, fearing that it somehow contradicts Wesley's (and by extension, God's) calls for humility and self-denial. But Wesley makes it clear in this sermon that pleasure should not be completely rejected as sinful but can indeed lead us to God. A queer embrace of pleasure as a byproduct of love is an essential mark of holiness, and Holiness churches would do well to open themselves to this aspect of it rather than shutting themselves off from it. True and unselfish love—and its byproduct, pleasure—is always a mark of holiness. Therefore, if churches reject queer love, they incidentally reject a Wesleyan understanding of holiness in the process. To condemn queer pleasure and queer love is not to champion holiness but to deny it.

Conclusion

If Søren Kierkegaard identified holiness as purity of the heart, that is, to will one thing, we might say that Wesley identifies holiness as circumcision of the heart, to will queer things. Inasmuch as circumcision of the heart is queer, holiness is queer, and we can read Wesley's understanding of holiness as urging us toward a love as expansive and unlimited as God's in Christ. The markers of the circumcision of the heart that Wesley recognizes as holiness—humility, faith, hope, and love—all might point together toward a rather queer existence. If humility is right judgment of ourselves, it might actually look more like Elizabeth Edman's queer pride, and it might call the church's heteronormative powers to account and to repent. Faith revels in the risk and uncertainty of God's queer creation and calls the church to see this creation with queer eyes that trust in God rather than our own supposed sight. Queer hope rethinks what discipline looks like in holiness, grounding it on the hope of what God does in our lives rather than how "good" we can be, and calls the church to embrace the joy of God's provision and transformation of hearts here and now rather than forcing people to conform to an untenable, constantly deferred moral ideal. Love is the ultimate marker of holiness, and queer love—as well as pleasure—is as much an expression of holiness as heterosexual love can be. Queer love challenges the church to practice what it preaches and truly embrace all people and all loves as emblematic of the holiness that they display. Holiness is ultimately the marker of Christian life—a life that declares the inbreaking of the queer kingdom of God in which the mighty are cast down, the rich are sent away, and the exalted are humbled, in which, perhaps, the normative have received their reward, but the queer shall be abundantly blessed.

CHAPTER FOUR

Between the Encounter with Others and the Other

The Renewing Experience of Divine Grace and Its Problems

Pablo Guillermo Oviedo

Keywords: mission, identity, Protestant principle, grace, personal and social sanctification, intersubjectivity, Argentinian Methodism, feminist theology

Introduction

Considering that Wesleyan theology has been defined as a robust theology of God's grace, and taking into account the global crisis in which we are living, marked by imperial subjectivity with consequences of misfortune for people and the planet, I would like to discuss how we can renew ourselves as ecclesial communities of grace. Starting from these presuppositions, one of the most common ethical and practical problems in the experience of grace and in the mission of ecclesial communities is the fundamental relationship between our practice of personal piety and our connection with other human beings—in biblical terms, with our neighbors and their culture, their being an "other." For theology in general—and for Latin American theology in particular—the problem of "the other" (human) has been one of its fundamental aspects. In this work I propose to lay out how the inseparable relationship between the divine Other and human others is an inescapable challenge with great implications for our theology, the Wesleyan movement, and for Latin American Christianity.

Contextual Considerations

When we speak of Latin American Protestantism, and of Methodism within it, based on a theological and sociological analysis, we cannot fail to mention that it finds itself in a crisis of identity, meaning, and mission.[1] Evangelical churches will also have an important place in this conversation. The Latin American religious landscape is complex, dynamic, and diverse in its demands and in what it offers. The question is: How will churches understand their presence and their mission in these new historical crossroads among our people?

Latin America encounters a Protestant crisis in a context of cultural fragmentation, described by the recently deceased Brazilian Liberation theologian Vítor Westhelle: "The crisis of Latin American Protestantism is precisely this one: it oscillates between adapting to the situation instituted and becoming a supplementary institution without charisma or becoming a charismatic extreme without formative power. The first

1 Vítor Westhelle, *Voces de protesta en América Latina* (Mexico City: LSTCH, 2000), 98–99. See Alvarez Carmelo, "¿Hacia un nuevo protestantismo en América Latina y el Caribe?" in *Protestantismo y Cultura en América Latina,* ed. Tomás Gutierrez (Quito: CLAI-Cehila, 1994), 269–77. In the Latin American reality, religion, far from disappearing in this change of era, will continue to occupy an important place. The search for a horizon of meaning in some transcendent way continues to occur, albeit with a plurality of horizons. The crisis of confidence in Western culture reinforces the need for religion in both middle and high sectors, as well as in marginalized sectors. Whether as a provider of feeling, as a re-enchantment of the world that allows life to be sacralized, or as an experience of ecstasy, religion in Latin America will continue to occupy a key place.

is the trend observed among historical churches. The second is the case of Pentecostalism."[2] This forces us to mention the definition that Paul Tillich gives of the Protestant principle: "The Protestant principle, a name derived from the 'protestant protest' directed to counteract the decisions of the Catholic majority, contains the divine and human protests against any absolute demand regarding a relative reality, and opposes it even when it is carried out by a Protestant Church. The Protestant principle is the judge of all religious or cultural reality."[3] When we speak of grace and the Protestant principle in our Latin American context, we start from this difficulty of incarnation and inculturation in Protestantism, which challenges our Wesleyan theologies and communities in their mission.

Therefore, I will first present Wesley's theology as a theology of divine grace in relation to God and especially to our neighbor—personal and social sanctification—and how, from the encounter with others, we are renewed. Then we will briefly analyze how this problem has been key in Latin American liberation theology and philosophy and in the present moment. Then we will see how it has been and continues to be a pastoral problem exemplified in Argentinian Methodism, presenting missionary, ecclesial, and theological challenges, such as the reality of gender inequality. It is in this context of fluid relationships marked by exclusion, individualism, and consumerism that we ask ourselves: What can we contribute from Wesleyan theology in light of these ethical and social challenges? What call does the Spirit of Jesus make to us in our world?[4] We believe that the debate on this theme can illuminate our

---

2 Westhelle, *Voces de protesta en América Latina*, 100. However, it is precisely Protestantism, given that it has the initial experience of the cleavage in the asymmetric relationship between principle and form, which can give us the hope of resolving the disturbing split in Latin American cultural formation. Protestantism still belongs to the promising territory that lies between the extremes of charisma and power, linking the poles without identifying them.

3 Paul Tillich, *La Era Protestante* (Buenos Aires: Paidós, 1965), 245–46.

4 Walter Klaiber and Manfred Marquardt, *Viver a Graca de Deus, un compendio de Teologia Metodista* (São Bernardo do Campo: Editeo / São Paulo: Cedro, 1999), 178.

spiritual, theological, and missionary journey. It will also serve in the renewal and transformation of the Wesleyan communities, if we want to be faithful to the work that God is doing in our midst, as Wesley liked saying: to the extension of his reign of grace and justice.

Wesleyan Theology as a Theology of Grace: Encounter with the Other and the Others

Many have claimed that one of the hallmarks of Wesleyan theology is the experience of divine grace. "Wesleyan theology is a full theology of grace," says Richard Heitzenrater.[5] And Wesley, as a theologian of grace, with an inclusive and encompassing concept and an emphasis on sanctification, returns to the believer his responsibility before the God of grace. Albert Outler, in his classic work on Wesley's theology, observed that "for Wesley, the initiative of the Spirit is the dynamic essence of all grace." Years later, in his monumental edition of Wesley's sermons, he states bluntly: "The heart of Wesley's gospel was always a very vivid sense of grace working at all levels in creation and in history, in people and in communities. . . . The 'Catholic substance' of Wesley's theology (which includes the Protestant and the Catholic, the Western and the Eastern) is the theme of participation—the idea that all life is grace and all grace is the mediation of Christ by means of the Holy Spirit."[6] Theodore Runyon, in his most representative and up-to-date work of Wesleyan theology, reaffirms this same conclusion: "The key to all of Wesley's soteriological doctrines is his understanding of God's

5 Richard Heitzenrater, *Wesley and the People Called Methodists* (Nashville: Abingdon, 1995), 290.

6 Albert C. Outler, ed., *John Wesley* (New York: Oxford University Press, 1964), 33; *The Works of John Wesley*, Bicentennial Edition, ed. Albert C. Outler (Nashville: Abingdon, 1984), vol. 1, Sermons I, 98–99. Outler adds: "Wesley did not naturally invent any of these ideas, but neither did he find them joint and integrated in the special way that he tried and achieved to a large extent."

grace."[7] For Runyon, interpreting Wesley's theology for the present means emphasizing that it identifies the essence of Christianity as the renewal of creation and creatures through the renewal of the image of God in humanity.[8] He also interprets this renewal of the divine image as the axial theme of Wesley's soteriology. Therefore, the cosmic drama of the renewal of creation begins with the renewal of the image of God in humanity.

Despite the importance in Martin Luther's own experience of the doctrine of justification by faith, which was mediated by the Moravians, Wesley distances himself from the identification of salvation with justification alone, insisting that the "great salvation" is not completed before the renewal of the original vocation for which humanity was created: to live as the image of God in the world.[9] For citizens of the twenty-first century who are concerned about the environment, he warns about a fundamental point of the divine purpose: the salvation of the human being is a recovery of the original vocation, which is to be responsible for the administration of creation and cocreator of the new creation in the Spirit of Christ. Or as Runyon reinterprets the essence of Christianity from a Methodist perspective: the renewal of creation, through the renewal of the image of God in humanity. In this eschatological approach to Wesleyan thought, we can see that by discerning God's original intention for creation in the perspective of the "end times" (contrary to the Calvinist approach, which understands that all history is determined before creation), "new possibilities open continually (in current history) through the creative power of the Holy Spirit."[10]

---

7 Theodore Runyon, *A Nova Creaçao: A Teologia de Joâo Wesley Hoje* (São Bernardo do Campo: Editeo, 2002), 39. See also *Works of John Wesley,* 1:98.

8 Runyon, *A Nova Creaçao,* 16. See Wesley's sermon 44, "Original Sin," in *Works of John Wesley,* 1:292.

9 Runyon, *A Nova Creaçao,* 21. See chap. 6, "Wesley para os dias de hoje: Os cuidados com o meio ambiente," 250–58.

10 Ibid., 17. Cf. Henry H. Knight III, *The Presence of God in the Christian Life: John Wesley and the Means of Grace* (Metuchen, NJ: Scarecrow, 1992), 73.

In relation to the means of grace and renewal, according to José Míguez Bonino, "Wesley refuses to dissociate the elements that represent both traditions: the objective elements that represent the Protestant tradition (the Word, the sacraments and the order) and the subjective elements that represent the pietist tradition (experience, inner holiness, meditation, spontaneous prayer, fraternal communion)."[11] In other words, he theoretically rejects all privatizing tendencies of the sanctification of the Spirit and all individualist "enthusiasm," which, instead of building community, divides it. Instead he emphasizes tradition, order in worship, and the unity of the church.

But we can also recover the disposition of constant surprise in the light of the freeing actions of the Holy Spirit, in the "great and extraordinary work" that God is doing among us, in times of deep changes and of a phenomenal "undoing" in the life of his people.[12] It is in this context that Wesley makes use of the work of the Spirit as the one who unites what is divided, rescues the rejected, and restores the love and unity of the community.

Míguez Bonino also warns us that renewal and mission are inseparable, which is why it is necessary to rethink the totality of the church in light of the incarnation of the Son, since we will clash with Wesley's spiritualism and individualism that were common in his time. Míguez Bonino comments that "the Wesleyan Christ sometimes seems only concerned in souls little connected with his concrete reality, due to his weak doctrine of the humiliation of the Christ and his earthly life."[13] This perception glimpses the possibilities that are opened in history by

---

11 José Míguez Bonino, *Hacia una eclesiología evangelizadora: Una perspectiva Wesleyana* (San Pablo: Editeo-Ciemal, 2003), 72. The ecclesiola or the bands were his way of linking these two currents in practice.

12 J. Gonzalez, *Wesley en América Latina* (Buenos Aires: Aurora, 2004), 84–85. He says: "To let God do, to do theology where God is acting, what I called theology on horseback."

13 Míguez Bonino, *Hacia una eclesiología evangelizadora,* 78. See also John Deschner, *Wesley's Christology: An Interpretation* (Dallas: Southern Methodist University Press, 1960), 2.

the creative force of the Spirit. For us today, the implication is that with its sanctifying air, the Spirit wishes to renew, in its agapic communion, all creation in Christ: human beings, society with its structures, and the whole of nature.

Taking into account this general framework, we focus on the praxis of grace, that is, on the relationship between the means of grace and our spirituality: between works of piety and works of mercy. In a recent contribution that problematizes this topic, Joerg Rieger says:

> A new reflection on the works of mercy as a means of grace can help us overcome the old impasse that has led to the traditional division between Orthodoxy and orthopraxis. Placing together both works of piety and mercy as the means of grace, Wesley manages to join the love of the Other (divine) and the other (human) in a special way that deserves to be analyzed in detail. This challenges not only Methodism but contemporary Christianity as a whole. Could it possibly be the fact that the relationship of the Divine Other cannot be separated from the relationship with the human other and, in this way, it helps to overcome one of the most damaging and paralyzing impasses of the Church today?[14]

An example of how Wesley puts this to practice is when he says that "religion must not go from the greatest to the least, or the power would

---

14 Joerg Rieger, *Gracia bajo presión* (Buenos Aires: Aurora 2015), 49. The author mentions in this edition in Spanish (p. 9) that chapter 1 of this book is in an earlier version in English: see "What Do Margins and Center Have to Do with Each Other? The Future of Methodist Traditions and Theology," in *Methodist and Radical: Rejuvenating a Tradition*, ed. Joerg Rieger and John J. Vincent (Nashville: Kingswood Books, 2003); and chapter 2 in its basic ideas are in English in Rieger, "Between God and the Poor: Rethinking the Means of Grace in the Wesleyan Tradition," in *The Poor and the People Called Methodist*, ed. Richard Heitzenrater (Nashville: Kingswood Books, 2003).

appear to be of men."[15] Now let us see how this is expressed in Latin American theology.

The Problem of "the Other" in Latin American Theology and Philosophy

The topic of "the other" has been one of the greatest problems of Latin American theology—both Catholic and Protestant—and it continues to be a point of discussion. Speaking from his Wesleyan heritage, Míguez Bonino commented on how religious individualism and egocentrism marked evangelical theology and spirituality. Among broad sectors of Latin American evangelical Protestantism, he found an "individualist, Christological-soteriological space in a basically subjective key with an emphasis on sanctification."[16]

Additionally, Vítor Westhelle states that "one of the great difficulties of Latin American theology has been the problem of the other." He goes on to say:

> Like Latin American literature, having inherited the European paradigms, theology must assert itself, presenting another question, and specifically the question of what the other is within the theological construction. By locating this other among the poor—or the victims—who have become invisible, and constructing the subjectivity of the non-person, theology points towards the implosion of inherited models. And this is the ironic task of theology within the rhetoric of official Christianity.[17]

---

15 Cf. John Wesley, *Works,* ed. Thomas Jackson, 3rd ed. (London: Wesleyan Methodist Book Room, 1872), 3:178.

16 José Míguez Bonino, *Rostros del protestantismo latinoamericano* (Buenos Aires: Nueva Creacion, 1995), 46.

17 Westhelle, *Voces de protesta en América Latina,* 54. Westhelle argues that Bartolomé de las Casas was a pioneer in this task of recognizing otherness in Latin American theology in the sixteenth century, in the midst of the harshness of Spanish colonialism. Also see from the same author, "Re(li)gión, the Lord of

In this way, an autonomous doctrine of creation, separate from a Trinitarian framework, transforms one's own ethnicity and culture into something immutable and closed that can only conceive one's relationship with the other to be useful for ecclesial purposes. At the other extreme, an autonomous doctrine of redemption, without a holistic Trinitarian framework, reduces the human being to a sinner without name, land, people, culture, or family, and in the subjective and individualistic version that has affected us so much as Protestants, a human being turns into a person without body or community.

The theological task then, starting from the criticism of liberal modernity and ethical-relativistic tendencies of postmodernity, is to allow for us to encourage a transformation that occurs from that recognition of "otherness" and to receive a religious-sacred meaning in one's own space, because in its limit the other becomes epiphanic.

From Roman Catholicism, the Latin American theologian Juan Luis Segundo poses the problem of the other by connecting it with our unshaped idea of God, in his work *Our Idea of God.* He provides a renewed Trinitarian understanding of God, surpassing both the earliest monarchical forms of Christianity (modalism, subordinationism) and the later Western theism of the Enlightenment. These models are not naive because, as Segundo argues in the introduction to this book: "Precisely, because in deforming God we protect our egoism, our falsified and inauthentic ways of dealing with our brothers make close alliance with our falsifications of the idea of God. Our unjust society and our deformed idea of God form a terrible and intricate pact."[18] These

---

History and the Illusory Space," in *Region and Religion: Land, Territory, and Nation from a Theological Perspective*, ed. Viggo Mortensen (Geneva: Lutheran World Federation, 1994), 82, 94–95. The expulsion of Jews and Muslims from the Iberian Peninsula coincides with the arrival of Europeans in the Americas and their inability to see the natives as humans outside their own frame of reference. See Vítor Westhelle, *After Heresy: Colonial Practice and Post-colonial Theologies* (Eugene, OR: Cascade Books, 2007), 15–32.

18 Juan Luis Segundo, *Teología Abierta para el laico adulto (tomo 3): Nuestra idea de Dios* (Buenos Aires: Lohlé, 1969), 13.

"atheistic" or "idolatrous" images of the Christian God have terrible consequences on Christian existence and on their dialogue with the world. This was illustrated by an Argentine folk singer and poet, Atahualpa Yupanqui, when he said: "That God cares for the poor, maybe he does, maybe he doesn't, but surely he has lunch at the owner's table."[19]

In Latin American philosophy, Enrique Dussel offers a perspective on modernity, globalization, and exclusion, expanding our perspective by stating that in order to understand Eurocentric modernity, we must recognize it as an instrument of coloniality toward the so-called Third World.[20] Dussel maintains—coinciding with Emmanuel Levinas and Kurt Appel—that ethics is prior to philosophical ontology. He elaborates:

> The other will be the other woman/man: a human being, an ethical subject, the face as an epiphany of living human

19 Atahualpa Yupanqui, in his poem and song "Questions about God." In Spanish: *Preguntitas sobre Dios*, a studio album released in 1969 in France by the Chant du Monde label (LDX 74415).

20 Enrique Dussel, *Globalización, Exclusión y Democracia en América Latina* (Mexico City: Contrapuntos, 1997), 91–92, 96–98. In this regard, Dussel declares that modernity entered the twentieth century, after five centuries of development, in a deep crisis, and that this crisis is not exclusive of Europe but a phenomenon of the world population. In the present time, the absolute limits have reached their maximum, such as the ecological destruction of the planet, because in modernity the environment was seen only as a means of production; we also face the destruction of humanity itself, since today we see that misery is the law of modernity and postmodernity. And finally there is the impossibility of restoring all those nations, economies, peoples, and cultures that modernity attacked so harshly in its origins and continues to exclude and corner in misery. Another author who writes on the same subject is Walter Mignolo, who insists on talking about modernity only in conjunction with coloniality, dividing the terms with a bar: "modernity/coloniality." There is a "double edge," he writes, in the "coexistence and intersection of modern colonialisms and colonial modernities." Walter D. Mignolo, *Coloniality, Subaltern Knowledges, and Border Thinking: Local Histories / Global Designs* (Princeton, NJ: Princeton University Press, 2000), 3.

> corporeality. . . . In the victim dominated by the system or excluded, the concrete human subjective empirical subjectivity is revealed as an interpellation, it is the interpellation of the one who exclaims I am hungry! Give me something to eat please! The Other is the possible victim caused by my functional action in the system. I am responsible.[21]

Wesleyan Theology from the Margins: An Alternative Intersubjectivity from a Christology from Below

Among other recent Wesleyan voices, who seek an alternative subjectivity from an encounter with the suffering others, Néstor Oscar Miguez, Joerg Rieger, and Jung Mo Sung's *Beyond the Spirit of Empire* offers new theological perspectives on politics and religion. The authors argue that the ethos of postmodernity, in which the battles between individualism and community occur, does not help to solve this dilemma since it questions subjectivity precisely at a time when marginalized people are winning it. They do not speak of subjectivity in general but of the subjectivity that emerges in the margins and that therefore places us on a different path. They affirm that we have to pay attention to what is really happening at the base, since this gives us a clearer understanding of the fact that even in the conditions of postmodern or postcolonial empire, the oppressed retain a kind of subjectivity and capacity for action.[22]

---

21 Enrique Dussel, *Etica de la Liberación en la edad de la Globalización y de la Exclusión* (Madrid: Trotta, 1998), 524.

22 Néstor Oscar Miguez, Joerg Rieger, and Jung Mo Sung, *Beyond the Spirit of Empire* (London: SCM, 2009). The authors refer to Rieger's book *Christ and Empire: From Paul to Postcolonial Times* (Minneapolis: Fortress, 2007), chap. 7, in which he introduces the term "postcolonial empire," which at first glance seems to be a paradox. In this book, a new Christology is worked from below, where the author seeks to reclaim Paul's notion of the lordship of Christ; the insistence of the complete divinity of Christ and humanity developed in the Councils of Nicea and Chalcedon; the notion of Anselm of the human God;

There are aspects of the divine that cannot be controlled by the empire and that continue to reappear despite the efforts of the system to subdue them. Rieger calls this a "theological surplus" or a "Christological surplus."[23] To affirm that Jesus Christ is a Lord, for instance, who was merciful to the marginalized is a challenge that continues to cause disturbance.

If the subjectivity of people cannot be totally controlled, why should we assume that there is a divine reality that can be? This is one of the fundamental keys of *Beyond the Spirit of Empire,* which is developed in each chapter. The difference is that this alternative type of surplus occurs in the reverse of history. Unlike dominant reality—the way in which the world is perceived from the hegemonic perspective—an alternative reality expresses the pain of common repression that creates new forms of solidarity and alternative subjectivities and activity. There is also another aspect that should not be overlooked, and it is how something new is produced that is not part of the system ("it is in the world but it is not of the world," paraphrasing John 17:6–19) but makes a difference.[24] Subjectivity and social action produce positive alternatives that create what realism and the dominant religion never understood as possible. We must not forget that these alternatives hold an opening that cannot be found in the dominant system and therefore can never ultimately be immobilized. Finally, the new forms of intersubjectivity that emerge here form the basis of a new humanity. In the words of Jung Mo Sung: "When one manifests and experiences the resistance to oppressive relations, one can recognize oneself as a subject

---

the notion of Bartolomé de Las Casas of the Way of Christ; the appropriation of Christ by Friedrich Schleiermacher as prophet, priest, and king, Christus Victor de Aulén; and the Cosmic Christ of Mateo Fox. Another exalted work is Michael Nausner's "Homeland as Borderland: Territories of Christian Subjectivity," in *Postcolonial Theologies: Divinity and Empire,* ed. Catherine Keller, Michael Nausner, and Mayra Rivera (St. Louis, MO: Chalice, 2004), 118–32.

23 For these terms see Rieger, *Christ and Empire.*

24 John Beverley, *Subalternity and Representation: Arguments in Cultural Theory* (Durham, NC: Duke University Press, 1999), 103.

and, at the same time, recognize the subjectivity of other people beyond any and all the social roles. It is the experience of gratuity in a face-to-face relationship."[25]

The new relationship that is constructed by those who embody an alternative subjectivity allows a face-to-face encounter that is not possible in a system in which subjectivity depends on power differences, that is, in which the subject can only be understood as subjecting others and placing them under monitoring—an understanding that often perpetuates notions of "leadership" promoted not only in the business world but also in politics and the church. Here we see a transcendental moment, because these new forms of intersubjectivity cannot be manufactured or controlled, and they push beyond any existing system.

This is a "true spiritual experience of grace and justification by *faith* that *justifies* the existence not only of the oppressed person, but also the one that feels indignation."[26] This kind of justification—a way of realizing God's justice that opposes the empire's notion of justice, as Christianity discovered at the beginning of the Roman Empire—may still be the best antidote to the automatic subjection to capitalism. Alternative desire is at the heart of alternative subjectivity. This alternative desire is, then, a true collective phenomenon and has the potential to create a new human condition. However, this alternative desire also needs to be organized. Without organization, it will disappear. This can be the

---

25 Jung Mo Sung, *Sujeto y sociedades complejas* (San José, Costa Rica: DEI, 2005), 63.

26 Sung, *Sujeto y sociedades complejas,* 233. This argument is further developed in Rieger, "Developing a Common-Interest Theology from the Underside," in *Liberating the Future: God, Mammon, and Theology*, ed. Joerg Rieger (Minneapolis: Fortress, 1998). Also see the excellent book edited by Miguel A. De La Torre and Stacey M. Floyd-Thomas, *Beyond the Pale: Reading Theology from the Margins* (Louisville, KY: Westminster John Knox, 2011), and the chapter in that book by Harold Recinos, "John Wesley" (95–103), in which he reflects on Wesley's experience in relation to the oppression of slavery. Also see Harold Recinos, "Barrio Christianity and American Methodism," in Rieger and Vincent, *Methodist and Radical*, 77.

wisdom incarnated in alternative religious movements and others when they are part of the reverse of history.

There is no middle way in this polarized situation of empire: "No one can serve two masters; for either he will hate the one and love the other, or he will esteem the one and despise the other. You cannot serve God and the rich," Jesus declares in Matthew 6:24 and Luke 16:13. Those who are in the middle are generally dragged in defense of existing powers in order to create a sense of stability, which is mostly illusory. But they can also choose to take a step back from this system that does not allow them to form alternative subjectivities and join the emergent relationships of base intersubjectivity. Many examples could be given.

How does this affect our theological understanding and our Christian mission? If we start from the renewing experience of grace in the Holy Spirit and not from the imperial spirit, life and mission should be carried out from the margins. An anthropology and subjectivity of grace is present from a Christology from below and from the margins. God's plan for the world is not to create another world but to re-create what God has already created in love and wisdom. Jesus began his ministry by affirming that being filled with the Spirit means freeing the oppressed, restoring sight to the blind, and announcing the coming of God's kingdom (Luke 4:16–18). He undertook the fulfillment of his mission by opting for those who were on the margins of society and rejecting a paternalistic focus on charity, because their situations testified to the sin of the world, and their longing for life was a part of God's design. Jesus Christ relates to and welcomes those who are most marginalized in society in order to challenge and transform everything that denies life, including cultures and systems that generate and maintain poverty, discrimination, and generalized dehumanization and exploit and destroy people and the earth.

The mission from the margins is a call to understand the complexities of power dynamics, systems and world structures, and local contextual realities. The Christian mission has sometimes been understood and practiced in ways that fail to recognize that God opted for those who are systematically pushed to the margins. Thus the mission from the margins invites churches to rethink the mission as a vocation inspired by the God's Spirit who works for a world in which the fullness of life is possible for everyone.[27] Let us consider an example of marches and countermarches of a specific pastoral case in relation to this topic of the encounter with others.

An Ecclesial Example of This Problem of the "Others": Argentinian Methodism

In the case of Methodism in Argentina and the larger Southern Cone, one of the characteristics that made it a dynamic and movement-oriented religious context was its capacity for intercultural diffusion and—in theological terms—to be incarnated in different historical moments in Argentina. What made the Methodist Church in Argentina (IEMA), in its missionary vision and practice, a missionary church that was committed and "embodied" sociopolitically between the 1960s and 1970s? What historical and theological factors made this change possible in its life and mission? The missionary conception of Wesleyan heritage led Argentinian Methodism to incarnate itself in different historical moments of its diffusion and expansion in response to the

27 See Kenneth R. Ross, Jooseop Keum, Kyriaki Avtzi, Roderick R. Hewitt, and Néstor Míguez, eds., *Juntos por la vida y la teología contemporánea latinoamericana*, vol. 3 of *Nuevas concepciones de misión y los cambios de contexto* (Buenos Aires: La Aurora, 2017). Nestor Míguez affirms: "The mission of the Christian faith today in Latin America is fourfold: it includes caring for and enjoying the goods of creation, working to build a worthy town, with agreements and conflicts, and engaging in the search for social and economic justice in the continent that supports the most unequal distribution of wealth and thus proclaim and live in open dialogue—with the others—original peoples, women and their voices and many other excluded—a testimony of our hope in the life that we receive through the grace of God the Creator, Jesus Christ the Messiah, and the life-giving breath of the Spirit, the community of the divine trinity that inspires the human community" (266).

challenges that its context presented.[28] In the larger view, preaching in Spanish first occurred in the context of Argentinian Methodism. It was one of the first evangelical churches in the country that integrated more Spanish and Italian immigrants—foreigners to Methodism's English origin—and "Criollos" in the transition from the nineteenth to the twentieth century.

Argentinian Methodism made a key contribution with its social ethic to the formation of liberal democratic laws and the establishment of a secular, free, and public system of national education in Latin America. Until the second half of the twentieth century, these contributions were theologically oriented from the *countercultural model*[29] that was predominant in Latin American Protestantism, which considers culture as an enemy that must be redeemed. Conversely, the revolutionary atmosphere that developed in Latin America between the 1960s and 1970s—a *kairos* moment that made Latin America a sociocultural, political, and religious "laboratory" in the second half of the twentieth century[30] and led to the emergence of Latin American liberation theology—produced profound changes in the management and laity of much of the IEMA, causing the consequent institutional autonomy and redesign of its missionary strategy in all areas.

These changes partially broke with the inherited liberal and conservative theological and institutional model and initiated steps toward autonomy in the national and Latin American context. Methodism from Argentina and the Río de la Plata region contributed great leaders

---

28 Various theological traditions shaped the theological ideology of the IEMA, including original Methodism, the traditions of the social gospel and liberal Protestantism of the nineteenth century, US evangelical conservatism, and the neo-orthodox Barthianism.

29 See Stephen Bevans, *Modelos de Teología Contextual* (Quito: Verbo Divino, 2004), 14. Also see Pablo G. Oviedo, "Análisis del discurso de la Iglesia Metodista Argentina en relación a la auto-comprensión de su tarea (1983–1989)," in *Revista Evangélica de Historia*, vols. 3–4 (Buenos Aires: AH-IEMA, 2005–6), 47.

30 Silva Gotay, *El pensamiento cristiano revolucionario en América Latina y el Caribe* (Salamanca: Sígueme, 1980), 17, 367–69.

to Latin American liberation theology and to the regional ecumenical movement in the Latin American Council of Churches (CLAI) in 1982, as well as to the World Council of Churches. As Stephen Bevans says, "contextual theology is done when the experiences of the past are committed to the present context."[31] In that sense, the praxis model was the one that the IEMA began to experience consciously. It emphasized the prophetic tradition of Christianity and the obedient following of Jesus, demonstrating that in the lives of the poor and excluded, he called from his Spirit to act without delay in that context.[32]

At the close of the twentieth century and beginning of the twenty-first, the IEMA has entered into a general rethinking of its life and mission due to the crisis of mission that it began to experience. In this regard, Andiñach and Bruno speak of expanding the church with new congregations, of producing changes in theological education, of reforming its organizational structures, and of reviewing service projects. These changes occurred not only because of the need for security and certainty that society, at the end of the century, did not offer, but also as a reaction to crisis situations where many church members have suffered the impoverishment of the middle class. Reflecting its middle-class majority in its ideological reflexes and cultural characteristics, the IEMA has generated a certain passive resistance to projects destined to the lower classes, which continues being the focus of Methodist mission. Perhaps this is why the classic projects of evangelization are more appealing as a way of holding onto "safe" actions in the midst of the crisis.[33]

31 Bevans, *Modelos de Teología Contextual,* 15.

32 Ibid., 13.

33 Pablo R. Andiñach and Daniel Bruno, *Iglesias Evangélicas y derechos humanos en la Argentina (1976–1998)* (Buenos Aires: La Aurora, 2001), 100. See the article by José Mîguez Bonino, "Una Iglesia en busca de sí misma: Un testimonio personal," *Revista Evangélica de Historia* 2 (2004): 141–58. Míguez Bonino speaks of the difficulties of the middle class of Argentine Methodism in the encounter with those who are different.

In the context of the neoliberal crisis that left the region in unprecedented levels of poverty at the beginning of the millennium, and with the subsequent appearance of a popular and neo-Keynesian political alternative in the economic sphere, the churches are now ecumenically reunited to face the challenges of rebuilding the country. With a slow democratic and economic recovery, beginning in 2007, Methodism resumed its tradition of public pastoralism, contributing to the atmosphere of popular participation and efforts to expand the individual and social rights that were achieved during that period. Different ethical issues, such as the subsequent law of equal marriage or the decriminalization of late-term abortion, are tensions that come in and out of discussion, due to differences in the understanding of the political participation of Christians. These ethical challenges have also highlighted the fundamentalism present in the diversity of religious traditions, challenging attempts at Christian unity.[34]

Again, I argue that the IEMA is confronted with the intercultural challenge of connecting with the new faces of the mission, the others that emerge in a new historical juncture now marked by the regional return of the neoliberal wave: women, children, youth, aboriginal peoples, people with different sexual identities, and so many others. Engagement with these others cannot come from paternalistic charity or using others as means to increase church membership. Instead, the IEMA must once again leave the confinement of religious egocentrism—as it did by God's grace in other times—toward the encounter of others, which today reveals the face of Christ on the margins, as the parable of the final judgment in Matthew 25 seems to imply.[35]

---

34 Daniel Bruno, "Abordaje y periodización para una historia del metodismo en Argentina," *Revista Evangélica de Historia,* no. 7 (2012): 41. And it has highlighted religious and political fascism in sectors of all the churches.

35 See José Míguez Bonino, "Methodism and Latin American Liberation Movements," in Rieger and Vincent, *Methodist and Radical,* 193.

Missionary and Theological Challenges: The Example of Feminist Theology

Responding to these challenges to our Wesleyan theology is undoubtedly a huge task. As an example, I can share what I experienced in an intercultural experience of Methodist connection: the evangelization seminar in July 2018 for the Latin American Southern Cone organized by the World Evangelism Institute of the Methodist World Council and the Methodist Churches of the Latin American Southern Cone.[36]

At this gathering, the voices of different marginalized groups emerged—the others—that challenge our churches in our Latin American context but also in other places. These others express the reality of exclusion and growing poverty with the return of neoliberal conservative governments in the region and especially the impact of these policies on children, adolescents, and women, among others.

Next, and as an example, I will briefly mention the challenge to our theology of women and their struggle for life. I believe that we must make visible the unjust, ruthless, and cruel reality that women experience in all dimensions of human life. Doing this is fundamental in the process that has been called the hermeneutic circle, starting from reality with all its rawness. Here socio-analytical mediation as an auxiliary source of theology is essential to be able to see and become aware, in this case of injustice and inequality in gender roles, to the detriment of women. In this sense, starting from the Latin American reality, it is essential to draw a panorama that does justice and makes visible this drama worldwide, from the perspective of feminist theologies. First, it is important to clarify that the reality that challenges me personally is the

36 Intercultural experiences in the Methodist system, such as the Oxford Institute of Methodist Theological Studies, are very important for networking. Michael Nausner explains how experiences with cultural boundaries can be understood as the main sources for Christian formation and how the connectional structure of global Methodism has the potential to provide an appropriate ecclesiastical format for these essential experiences. See "Intercultural Experience in the Methodist Connectional System," *Caminhando* 21 (2008): 87–96.

relationship with my wife and other women who are part of my friendships, my pastoral ministry, and my social context. The movement for women's rights in Argentina has been struggling for decades and has been made much more visible in the last three years by the increase in "femicide," the questioning of patriarchy as a structure, and the micromachismo of everyday life. I believe that this existential situation is the greatest moral dilemma and challenge—specifically for Christian faith and ethics—that we are going through in our Río de la Plata regional context. I specify Christian faith and ethics because it was the great challenge of the rights of the poor—those excluded and of the earth who are the general others—who proposed Latin American liberation theology as a theological and ethical challenge. The case of specificity has the added particularity of being transversal, since women suffer the ruthless power of capitalism and patriarchy with their cultural and religious legitimations. This reality has moved me in recent years and has made me aware of my contradictions, limitations, and complicities as a privileged male within the patriarchal system.

As for women, three religious "imaginaries" have been built in Latin America that serve as a justification for women's roles. These images are the immaculate virgin, the selfless mother, and the seductress/prostitute.[37] These three roles, as can be seen, define women only in terms of their sexual relationship with men, which reduce their value; the woman is not someone by herself but receives meaning from the male. Traditionally the macho Latin culture has found its backing in religion, allowing it to maintain a distortion of women as well as men. Therefore within ecclesial communities at least three different groups of women can be identified by the positions that they assume in response to this distortion.[38]

---

37 Irene Tokarski, "Equidad de género para un iglesia, teología y pastoral incluyentes," ISEAT, La Paz, 2010, 56.

38 These groups allow women to respond from where they are located, as Nancy Bedford argues in *La Porfía de la Resurrección. Ensayos desde el feminsimo Latinoamericano* (Buenos Aires: Kairós, 2008), 16. According to Bedford, a quick historical review of feminist hermeneutics and theology identifies three

First, there are those who abandon the faith after recognizing their place in history and see themselves as dignified, autonomous, and of age, coming to the conclusion that the Christian faith is such a heteronomous path that it is insufferable, and that it is impossible for them to be faithful to themselves and remain within the faith.

There is a second group that persists in love and commitment to faith, that chooses the path of alienation to survive in the face of the rigidity and authoritarianism of theologians and leaders who are in charge of maintaining the situation. These leaders consider that the problem is with women, and so they do not accept questions because they arise from women.

---

moments: The first arises in the midst of reflection on the theology of liberation, the popular movements, and the political struggles in which they find women, impelling them to read the Bible, in a search for a God that confirms the struggle for themselves and for their peoples. This moment seeks to identify and recognize female leaders in the Bible. In the second moment, the feminine dimensions of God are sought in the Bible, and the nonconformity is declared against the patriarchalism present in the theological discourse. God is Father but also Mother, but the limit of this moment is that there is a reduced vision of masculine and feminine identities; it is associated with the feminine as fragility, tenderness, affection. The relationship between the masculine and feminine is seen as complementary without any criticism of the cultural and historical construction of the roles assigned to both. The third moment, in which we find ourselves, is characterized by a search for a holistic theology, where the rigid patterns of masculine and feminine are questioned and it is proposed to overcome them. This implies an epistemological rupture, because it challenges us to think in a different way about identity and to know and therefore to build new relationships with the world, with people, and with God. This challenge leads us to open dialogue with differences, and here at least two important dialogues appear, urgent with culture and diversity. Elsa Tamez, writing on feminist Latin American hermeneutics, also identifies three periods: the decade of the seventies, focused on hermeneutics from the oppression of women; the eighties, focused on hermeneutics from the perspective of women; and the nineties, focused on hermeneutics from a feminism of liberation. See Tamez, *La sociedad que las mujeres soñamos: Nuevas relaciones varón-mujer en un nuevo orden económico* (San José: DEI, 2001), 167–71.

Finally, a third group recognizes that it is this same faith in Jesus Christ that leads them to recognize themselves as feminists, in the sense that it prompts them to reformulate their theologies from which transformative discourses emerge for both men and women. From this experience of being in Christ—free, autonomous, equal, and worthy—they assume the commitment to be disciples of Christ and to promote the Kingdom together with their brothers. The significant amount of physical and symbolic acts of violence toward women are not isolated incidents. In fact, it does not seem exaggerated to speak of femicide in our countries, that is, of a mass murder of women that seems to be tolerated collectively and sanctioned in practice by the prevailing legal and economic system.

Therefore, if the Gospel is opposed to violence—including rape and femicide—the church will necessarily have to defend gender equality. Here we must remember that equal is not the same as identical—equality is not about erasing particularities but about insisting on the task of breaking down what it means to affirm that men and women are carriers of the *imago Dei* concretely and materially in equal measure. In practice, this leads to the fact that if the church does not promote equality (for whatever reason and regardless of its good intentions), it ends up disguising gender violence and even promoting it. The exact contours of gender equality cannot be prescribed: it is necessary to imagine respectful and contextual ways of living it, making the way by walking. But the principle of the equality of men and women before God and in the world has to assume a leading role if theological anthropology is to contribute to building peace and justice instead of contributing to violence and injustice.

The fact is, then, that just as women who resist violence can sketch their critical path, with the help of the *ruach*, the Spirit of God, theological anthropology can do the same, in a multiplicity of contexts, situations, and cultures. We have to rethink Christology, from a Trinitarian hermeneutics and grace from below and from the margin, to do justice to the ultimate revelation of God in the specific and fully human person of Jesus of Nazareth. On this topic, God is deeply committed to particularity. God is incarnated in the particularity of a human being, so that we can (in all our particularities) share the very life of God (theosis). To suggest that a specific kind of human particularity (such as skin color or gender or sexuality) stands on top of all others is profoundly opposed to the liberating message of the Gospel. The use of symbolic or physical violence to impose domination and gender hierarchy is also opposed to the Gospel message, as Nancy Bedford suggests: "A theological anthropology that undertakes a critical path will need to imagine ways of respecting the particularity and to avoid the pitfalls of gender complementarity that are sometimes hidden in the margins of the doctrine of the *imago Dei*, even in its feminist versions."[39]

Recognizing the trauma of gender inequality and violence and of some of the conditions that lead to greater violence against women, some signs of hope are glimpsed in the actions of women and men who resist violence in nonviolent ways. What could be the role of theology and its ethics in general, and of a particular intercultural feminist theology, in the face of such reality? The development and promotion of a theological anthropology of grace—coherent with a Christology of grace—and the transformation of dominant subjectivity, capable of resisting violence against women, are key. A theological anthropology of this kind needs to be consciously freed from the explicit or implicit complicity with violence against women, striving to find a critical path that can contribute to their flourishing. In addition, we need to change the way we work in daily ecclesial life as well as in our theological task. In the Brazilian context, Nancy Pereira gives voice to this need, arguing that "the biggest problem is not only in the gender formation of a Methodist theology, but in a dramatic way, in the relations of power and gender within Brazilian Methodism—and in general."[40]

---

39 Bedford, *La Porfía de la Resurrección,* 85.

40 Nancy Cardoso Pereira, "Fragmentos e Cacos de Experiência 1: Relações sociais de poder e gênero na teología wesleyana," *Revista Caminhando,* 8, no. 2 (2003): 12.

By Way of Conclusion: Renewal in Grace from the Encounter with Others

The Spirit of Jesus, who acts particularly from below and from the margins, points us to a time in which an epoch is falling apart while simultaneously a new time is brewing. What paths should our theology and our communities follow to be renewed and transformed from the grace of Jesus, in relation to others who are in a world of disgrace? The cultural and theological reflections that I shared in this essay do not allow me to reach a final conclusion. Such a conclusion would limit the possibility of always being open to new faces of others that constantly question us in our life and mission. Seen through a theological-cultural lens, our encounters with others who are marginalized from the life of grace in Christ remind us of the continuous need for theological thinking—in this case, a Christology and human subjectivity from grace—and a plural hermeneutics that takes into account the perspectives of the different others who challenge our comfort and religious egocentrism.

In the logic of the grace of the kingdom of God, we know that in evangelizing we are evangelized, and in the genuine encounter with others and their crosses, we are renewed. This is our message: the power of death could not quench the faith, hope, and love that the Son of God manifested in his life and ministry. The one who died that shameful death was not gone for the women who prepared ointments and spices to care for the broken body, according to Luke. Only after performing an act of love and grace for a body that could not say a word of thanks will we find ourselves with the surprising renewal and liberation of our life. The only suffering that has meaning is that which we accept in the struggle against suffering. Therefore the definitive victory of God's love over sin and death, and the impossibility of the resurrection of Jesus, is not realized if it is not assumed and faces the terrible experience of pain, suffering, and the cross. In the words of Vítor Westhelle, "A theology of the cross is always found on the other side of the practice of the resurrection, and conversely:

a resurrection practice can only be exercised in the face of the fatal experience of the cross."[41]

Our praxis of the means of grace must be challenged to integrate this dangerous and subversive memory of the grace of Jesus of Nazareth, who from his humanity was able to lodge and stay, to be compassionate and merciful, to be transformed from the sacred encounter with the other. "Just as some have claimed for years that there is a need for a human socialism in Latin America, we must continue to seek a humanized Gospel and a humanized Methodism from the compassionate grace of Jesus."[42]

A cultural marker of Argentina and the Rio de la Plata region is the original drink of the Guaraní aborigines, the so-called *mate*. It is perhaps the most popular symbol of the intimate and genuine encounter with the other because of its inclusive and communitarian dimension.[43] In some churches, for years, *mate* has been shared in spaces where the means of grace are practiced: in biblical meetings and prayer in small groups, in the work of evangelization and *diakonia,* even in worship services. The *mate* as a group drink—a symbol of encounter and empathy—is given, shared, and received and includes the different, the new, and the marginalized. We need a Christianity, a Methodism—with the roots and face of *mate.*

What is needed is not only orthodoxy nor orthopraxis, but also an evangelical *orthopathy of grace* that transforms our ecclesial and cultural

41 Westhelle, *Voces de protesta en América Latina,* 126.

42 Fragment of the preaching of the bishop of the Methodist Church Argentina, Américo Jara, at the close of the International Training Seminar, organized by World Methodist Evangelism—CMM, in Buenos Aires, July 29, 2018.

43 It is also good to clarify that the rural worker, called *yerbatero,* and his family are exploited in a ruthless way. The *yerbatero* receives as the value of his work six Argentine pesos for a kilo of yerba leaf harvested, and the price in the supermarkets is seventy Argentine pesos. This is an unfair approximate difference of 11.5 times for each kilo. I send my appreciation to Timothy Eberhart for reminding me of this situation, in order to make visible the drama of the rural workers in Argentina, another example of the excluded that we are talking about in this essay.

subjectivities. Both theologically and culturally, I am challenged not to imagine a common future of our Wesleyan Methodist community and its local and global mission without the participation of those who have been excluded for centuries. This is nothing more and nothing less than our task, because we are convinced by his Spirit that from the passage of Jesus Christ through our history, "every act of love never ends without a future."[44]

44 José Míguez Bonino, *Espacio para ser hombres* (Buenos Aires: Aurora, 1990), 70.

CHAPTER **FIVE**

Grace under Pressure

Wesleyan Moves from Charity and Advocacy to Deep Solidarity

JOERG RIEGER

Keywords: grace, works of mercy, charity, advocacy, solidarity

Introduction

In the Wesleyan traditions, grace is often more readily experienced under pressure than on the mountaintops. The means of grace help illustrate this, in terms of John Wesley's concern to hold together the so-called works of piety and works of mercy. As a result, this chapter will argue that revival, reform, and revolution—the theme of the Oxford Institute of Methodist Theological Studies 2018—belong together inextricably and that current ecclesial models of charity and advocacy need to be complemented and reshaped by what I have been calling deep solidarity.

An earlier version of this chapter was presented at the Oxford Institute of Methodist Theological Studies in Oxford, England, in the summer of 2018.

Contextual Considerations

In the Wesleyan traditions, grace is often more readily experienced under pressure than on the mountaintops, a point I have made repeatedly in recent years.[1] In other words, grace is experienced more profoundly in the struggles of life than in occasional moments of triumph, elation, and ecstasy. Without taking experiences of grace under pressure into account, both Christian theology and praxis are easily distorted and misled, a problem that might explain in part the woes of Christianity in the United States today. In Wesleyan theology, grace under pressure is manifest in the various modes of grace: prevenient, justifying, and sanctifying. Prevenient grace helps people understand who they are in relation to God in the midst of the pressures of life, including a growing sense of their limitations and the reality of sin. Grace under pressure reminds us that sin is not just a personal matter but is manifest in distorted relationships within communities and the threats to the survival of millions of people and the planet. Next, justifying grace initiates a new relationship with God in the midst of pressure, and thereby with others, overcoming the injustices of distorted relationships that take both personal and structural forms. Sanctifying grace, finally, is the grace-driven effort to work through the pressures of life, beginning with the most severe forms, with the goal of overcoming sin in all its embodiments, personal and structural, local and global.

In all these manifestations, grace under pressure engages in struggles against sin and evil. It all begins with grace opening our eyes to the realities of sin and evil for the first time under prevenient grace and continues with an ever-deepening engagement of sin and evil as people move along the process of sanctification. As a result, grace is always engaged in the most profound pressures of the world; on the mountaintops it tends to make people feel better but rarely makes a difference in the real world.

---

1 Joerg Rieger, *Grace under Pressure: Negotiating the Heart of the Methodist Traditions* (Nashville: United Methodist General Board of Higher Education and Ministry, 2011); Portuguese and Spanish translations.

Means of Grace

A theological reflection on the Wesleyan means of grace helps illustrate this, keeping in mind John Wesley's concern to hold together the so-called works of piety and works of mercy. To recap a case I have made in more detail elsewhere, Wesley defines means of grace, in accordance with the Anglican Book of Common Prayer, as "outward signs, words, or actions ordained of God, and appointed for this end—to be the ordinary channels whereby he might convey to men preventing, justifying, or sanctifying grace."[2] In other words, means of grace are channels provided by God through which we experience God's grace. To put it in more contemporary language, means of grace are special points at which God connects with us and we connect with God. The purpose of the means of grace is the cultivation of our relationship with God and with others. Grace is, therefore, essentially a relationship, and because relationships are dynamic, Wesleyans believe that we can grow (as well as decline) in grace.

Thinking through the traditional Anglican list of the means of grace, which includes reading the Bible, prayer, and Holy Communion, in terms of relationship would be a fruitful exercise. After all, it is not just that we read the Bible; the Bible also reads us. In praying we not only speak but also listen, and Holy Communion is more about relationship with God and others than about miraculous transactions from the top down.[3] However, since space is limited, let me move on to the other aspect of Wesley's theology of the means of grace that has been neglected by the church.

The older Wesley broadens his notion of the means of grace by adding what he calls "works of mercy" to the traditional "works of piety" of reading the Bible, prayer, and Holy Communion. In a late sermon titled "On Zeal," first published in 1781, Wesley notes that works of mercy are also means of grace, aware that "this is not commonly adverted

2 John Wesley, "The Means of Grace," in *The Bicentennial Edition of the Works of John Wesley*, vol. 1, ed. Albert C. Outler (Nashville: Abingdon, 1984), 381.

3 For more detailed reflections, see Rieger, *Grace under Pressure.*

to."[4] Moreover, he gives them a special place: Whenever works of mercy interfere with works of piety, he argues, the former "are to be preferred." Wesley explains further that "even reading, hearing, prayer, are to be omitted, or to be postponed, 'at charity's almighty call'—when we are called to relieve the distress of our neighbour, whether in body or soul."[5] Here, grace under pressure enters the picture.

This inclusion of the works of mercy into the means of grace is different from the well-known distinction between the "instituted" and the "prudential" means of grace; works of mercy cannot be relegated to a secondary list of prudential means of grace.[6] That works of mercy belong to the core of the Wesleyan tradition is reflected in the central place of Wesley's General Rules, which in United Methodism belong to the nonnegotiable doctrinal standards. In the General Rules, works of piety ("attending upon all the ordinances of God") are mentioned last, while works of mercy come first (framed in terms of "doing no harm" and "doing good").[7]

In addition, Wesley clearly states that Methodists already in his own time have fallen from grace because they were not aware that

---

4 John Wesley, "On Zeal," in *Bicentennial Edition,* 3:313.

5 Ibid., 3:314.

6 For Wesley the works of mercy are not just prudential in the sense that they would be optional means of grace, which may or may not be used according to changing circumstances. Wesley's distinction between instituted and prudential means of grace does not apply here, because works of mercy are not listed in either category. Cf. John Wesley, "Minutes of Several Conversations between the Rev. Mr. Wesley and others, from the year 1744, to 1789," in *The Works of the Rev. John Wesley,* ed. Thomas Jackson, 3rd ed. (London: Wesleyan Methodist Book Room, 1872; reprinted Peabody, MA: Hendrickson, 1986), 8:323–24 (hereafter cited as *Works*). This is overlooked also by Henry H. Knight III, *The Presence of God in the Christian Life: John Wesley and the Means of Grace,* Pietist and Wesleyan Studies 3 (Metuchen, NJ: Scarecrow, 1992), 5.

7 For the General Rules of The United Methodist Church, see http://www.umc.org/en/content/the-general-rules-of-the-methodist-church. Accessed September 3, 2018.

works of mercy are genuine means of grace.[8] There were Methodists who read the Bible every day, prayed even more often, and attended Holy Communion as often as possible—good and solid church people that any pastor would welcome with open arms—but who still had fallen from grace because they neglected the works of mercy as means of grace. One can only wonder what Wesley might say about contemporary Methodism in this regard.

Adding works of mercy to the works of piety and making them an essential part of the means of grace can have far-reaching implications. Most important, works of mercy are now also ordained channels of God's grace and part of grace as a relationship. Works of mercy are not only social outreach but also what I keep calling "inreach," means by which we connect with God and with each other and through which God and others enter our lives. This is the fundamental issue that I will develop further in this chapter. Moreover, works of mercy serve as a constant reminder that grace is most powerfully experienced under pressure.

Perhaps the most important result of this constellation is that works of mercy and works of piety are now in a position to reshape each other. We see new aspects of works of piety from the perspective of practicing works of mercy, while practicing works of piety can help us deepen our involvement in works of mercy. Engaging in works of mercy opens up new encounters with the Bible, transforms how we pray, and reshapes our theology of Holy Communion. Works of mercy as means of grace also deepen our experience of prevenient, justifying, and sanctifying grace. Vice versa, reading the Bible, praying, and Holy Communion inform how we engage in works of mercy. These dynamic interactions, which will be developed in what follows, are what is missing from self-declared centrist approaches to Methodist theology that have profoundly influenced the church for several decades.[9]

---

8 Cf. John Wesley, "On Visiting the Sick," in *Bicentennial Edition*, 3:385.

9 The work of legendary Methodist theologian Albert C. Outler may serve as an example for such a centrist approach, picked up by Scott Jones, *United Methodist Doctrine: The Extreme Center* (Nashville: Abingdon, 2002).

Charity and Advocacy

What are the deeper implications of considering works of mercy as means of grace? At the most basic level, works of mercy might be understood in terms of charity. Charity is a time-honored way for Christians to respond to the pressures of the world, and Methodists since the days of John Wesley have been engaged in it. Arguably, charitable giving is how the majority of people of faith today believe they can make a difference. Many take it for granted that this is the most faithful response to the pressures of life.

No doubt, charity has done a lot of good, providing relief for hunger, homelessness, poverty, and many other pressures that people face. Yet charity is not the only and perhaps not even the most helpful response to experiences of pressure. Grace under pressure pushes further. To put it bluntly: Jesus preached good news to the poor and freedom for the oppressed rather than charity (Matt. 11:5, Luke 4:18). What is good news to impoverished and oppressed people? Is it to be recipients of handouts—or is it that they will no longer be poor and oppressed?

When understood in terms of the means of grace, our conception of charity as a work of mercy deepens, because it will have to be reconceived as a two-way street. As noted above, means of grace are channels of God's grace, and in this framework charity and works of mercy are not just about what Methodists do for others but also about what comes back to us. What comes back here, of course, is twofold: an encounter with the other person who is the recipient of a work of mercy and an encounter with God.

Encounters with others and with God open our eyes both for grace as well as for sin—such encounters help us see more clearly where the pressures are and what the underlying problems might be. For Wesley and the early Methodists, for instance, engaging with the working poor enabled them to understand some of the problems of early capitalism such as exploitation and sharply increasing inequality.[10] Charity,

10 See the account of Ted Jennings, *Good News to the Poor: John Wesley's Evangelical Economics* (Nashville: Abingdon, 1990).

therefore, is at its best when it begins to push beyond one-way streets. When the eyes of those who engage in charity are opened to what causes poverty and oppression, we move one step closer to the experience of grace under pressure. That this is a step in the right direction is confirmed by hitting a nerve. As Dom Hélder Câmara, a former Roman Catholic bishop from Brazil, put it: "When I give food to the poor, they call me a saint. When I ask why they are poor, they call me a communist."[11] Even seemingly harmless acts of charitable giving have the potential to open our eyes.

When the one-way street of charity begins to open up to a two-way street, we are led into deeper understandings of the pressures of life, and a deeper search for experiences of grace under pressure begins. Advocacy is often the next step after charity. By advocacy I mean speaking out against injustices that cause pressures and challenging them. Although this may come as a surprise to most Christians and even to some Methodists, advocacy can be understood as a more faithful approach to sin and evil than charity, as it deepens the experience of grace under pressure. Advocacy is solidly grounded in many religious traditions. Many of the Jewish prophets speak out against injustice in the name of God, challenging those who "trample on the poor and take from them levies of grain" (Amos 5:11), and many voices in the New Testament concur.

Mary, the mother of Jesus, speaks of God's advocacy when she proclaims that the God who lifts up the lowly pushes the powerful from their thrones and fills the hungry with good things while sending the rich away empty (Luke 1:52–53). Her inspiration is Hannah, the mother of the prophet Samuel (1 Sam. 2:1–10), recognized not only by Christians but also by Jews and Muslims. Jesus, following along these lines, blesses the hungry and the poor and challenges the rich and the full (Luke 6:20–25). To be sure, both the lowly and the powerful as

---

11 "Quando dou comida aos pobres, chamam-me de santo. Quando pergunto por que eles são pobres, chamam-me de comunista." Quoted in Zildo Rocha, *Helder, O Dom: uma vida que marcou os rumos da Igreja no Brasil* (Petrópolis: Vozes, 2000), 53.

well as the hungry and the rich are experiencing grace under pressure here, albeit in very different ways: those who are forced to endure the pressures experience liberation; those who cause pressures and contribute to them are challenged and prodded to change their ways. Grace under pressure is not "one size fits all."

Standing in this tradition, Wesley proclaims that the majority of people were poor not by their own fault but because they were pushed off their lands by wealthy landowners and then exploited in the factories of early capitalism.[12] Wesley's categorical opposition to slavery and his support for enslaved people provide another example for the prominent place of advocacy in the Methodist traditions. This kind of advocacy is closely linked with an understanding of the works of mercy as means of grace under pressure: advocacy for others grows out of a deepening concern for those for whom one advocates, a clearer view of understanding of what causes the pressures they experience, and a deeper engagement with the roots of these pressures—all with an eye to how God's grace is already at work under pressure. Advocacy, thus, grows out of a recognition that the one-way street of charity is not enough—a recognition shared by Wesley in many cases.

Advocacy, therefore, brings us one step closer to the experience of grace under pressure and good news to the poor. Instead of works of mercy, however, it might be more appropriate to talk about works of justice. Even though that terminology cannot be found in Wesley, it is clear that he was engaged in works of justice, as his engagement cannot be confined to charity and the giving of alms. Nevertheless, even advocacy remains limited and does not yet fully embody the insight that works of mercy are means of grace.

While a two-way street begins to emerge with advocacy and relationships between self, other, and God gain in importance when compared to charity, the relationship between those who advocate and those for whom they advocate is often still limited. Advocates tend to

12 In his "Thoughts on the Present Scarcity of Provisions" of 1772 (*Works,* 11:56–57), Wesley talks about various causes of poverty, including the monopolizing of farms by the "gentlemen farmers" and the luxury of the wealthy.

perceive themselves as standing above those for whom they advocate—sometimes assuming that they are the voice for others who presumably have no voice. This limits not only the effectiveness of advocacy and the relation to other people but also the depth of relationship with God, which is at the heart of the means of grace tradition.

Advocacy and works of justice that fail to fully embrace the means of grace tradition can lead to advocates overestimating their own power and neglecting the contributions of others and of God. Not surprisingly, advocates often act in patronizing fashion, as if they were in a position to solve the problems of others. In this way, they lose the community support necessary to bring change and tend to stifle the initiative of those for whom they advocate. In the end, advocates without community support often burn out and walk away, or they lower their expectations and return to models of charity, never really experiencing the full potential of grace under pressure.

Both charity and advocacy ultimately amount to reforms of the status quo, as they do not lead to the reconstruction of the deepest problems of the current situation. In this way, they miss crucial opportunities that might not only revive but revolutionize the church and the world. Unfortunately, in many places today in both church and world, charity and advocacy are the only models that are discussed.

Deep Solidarity

Considering works of mercy as means of grace requires a more holistic response. This is what I am calling "deep solidarity."[13] Deep solidarity includes both charity and advocacy, but it reaches further. The witness of Amos, Mary, Jesus, and even of John Wesley can also be interpreted

13 For a more extensive discussion of the term *deep solidarity*, see Joerg Rieger and Kwok Pui-lan, *Occupy Religion: Theology of the Multitude* (Harrisburg, PA: Rowman and Littlefield, 2012). See also Joerg Rieger and Rosemarie Henkel-Rieger, *Unified We Are a Force: How Faith and Labor Can Overcome America's Inequalities* (St. Louis, MO: Chalice, 2016).

in this way. In what follows, I will argue that talking about works of solidarity captures the deeper theological meaning of the Wesleyan concept of works of mercy as means of grace.

To begin with, deep solidarity is more profoundly relational than either charity or advocacy. Unlike charity and advocacy, deep solidarity is not a matter of the more privileged supporting the less privileged; neither is it about solving the problems of other people. Deep solidarity is a matter of realizing our deep connectedness with others and with God, that the pressures that affect others might be affecting all of us in some ways, and that nothing will change unless we are facing the pressures of the world together and unless we experience grace under pressure together. Theologically speaking, this requires a more profound doctrine of sin and a more profound doctrine of grace than many of our theologies have to offer.[14]

Those who are experiencing the pressures of our time most severely—like for instance the many children whose families (including minority and nontraditional families and single parents) have trouble making ends meet even in the United States[15]—can help us see how sin is distorting all of our lives. Sin, in its most basic theological meaning, is the fracturing of relationships with God and with others, and this affects not only the poorest of the poor. Even the middle class is increasingly pulled into this fracturing of relationships and forced to endure the precariousness of existence and the pressures of our times in new and challenging ways—jobs are downgraded in a gig economy, health care and retirement move out of reach, and the

14 For the theological background of the relation of sin and salvation in Methodist theology, see Joerg Rieger, ed., *No Religion but Social Religion: Liberating Wesleyan Theology* (Nashville: United Methodist General Board of Higher Education and Ministry, 2018).

15 Twenty-one percent of all children in the US are living below the poverty line, with 43 percent in low-income families that often have trouble making ends meet. See the National Center for Children in Poverty, http://www.nccp.org/topics/childpoverty.html. Accessed July 24, 2018.

American Dream is dead for current and future generations.[16] In addition to all of this, all bets are off as climate change is already creating unprecedented damage.

As we deepen our relationships with others and with God under pressure, we find that our stories are often connected. What is happening at work may serve as an example: "mean and lean production" is practiced today not only in blue-collar factories but also in white-collar settings and even in universities and churches; likewise, low-wage work depresses all wages, and widespread reductions of benefits and violations of worker rights are creeping into all job sectors. All these pressures are rising, and they are further compounded by race, ethnicity, gender, sexuality, and mounting challenges of deportation and the associated separation of families.[17]

Mary, the mother of Jesus, provides an example of deep solidarity in the Christian tradition. Instead of speaking for the lowly ones of the world, she recognizes that she is one of them, and she takes sides (as liberation theologians realized decades ago, even the poor need to make an option for the poor). In so doing, she finds a deeper relation to God, who raises up the lowly and pushes the powerful from their thrones (Luke 1:52). Jesus, unlike many of his followers, remains conscious of his lowly beginnings as a construction worker born in a barn, and he never renounces his roots. His ministry takes place among people under pressure, in deep solidarity with them and in deep solidarity with God ("As you, Father, are in me and I am in you, may they also be in us, so that the world may believe that you have sent me" [John 17:21]).

The prophet Amos, a shepherd, likewise does not hesitate to side with those who are getting a raw deal in his time—and his concern is not merely the fracturing of human relationships but also the

---

16 For a reflection on what is now called the "precariat," see Guy Standing, *The Precariat: The New Dangerous Class* (New York: Bloomsbury Academic, 2016).

17 This has been the depressing news in the United States in the summer of 2018, when the Trump administration started to separate even young children of immigrants from their parents.

relationship with God ("For thus says the Lord to the house of Israel: Seek me and live" [Amos 5:4–5]). In their own ways, Mary, Jesus, and Amos embody deep solidarity in situations of tremendous pressure, and they realize, with the Apostle Paul, that "if one member suffers, all suffer together with it" (1 Cor. 12:26). The experience of grace under pressure goes deep and requires not only works of mercy and works of justice but works of solidarity as means of grace. As I will show, Wesley himself is after solidarity, although he does not use this term.

An ancient embodiment of deep solidarity can be found in the stories of Moses, whom all three Abrahamic religions (Judaism, Christianity, and Islam) hold in high esteem. Raised as an Egyptian prince, Moses wakes up when he finds himself in a situation of pressure, observing Hebrew slaves being abused by their taskmasters. Later, having joined the workforce as a shepherd, he accepts the call to join the solidarity movement of God and the Hebrew slaves, working for liberation (Exod. 3:1–12). This might be the real miracle of the Burning Bush story: both Moses and God enter into deep solidarity with people under pressure (observing, listening, and experiencing it)—the miracle of a bush that burns and is not consumed pales in comparison. As a result, grace is experienced under pressure, and good news is brought to the poor and the oppressed.

In his own ways, Wesley was involved in deep solidarity as well. As a young man he traveled to the United States as a missionary, interested in learning "the true sense of the Gospel of Christ by preaching it to the Heathen." This included learning from the Natives how to simplify his own life and to learn the practice of the community of goods as described in the book of Acts.[18] While some of this reflects romantic (and soft colonial) ideas that Wesley maintained even after he returned to England (never having had an opportunity to engage with Native Americans), his attitude also reflects a genuine two-way street that is characteristic of the works of solidarity as means of grace: he notes challenges posed by others and calls for conversion of the self.

18 John Wesley, "Letter to a Friend" (1735), *Works*, 12:38.

The same is true for Wesley's reflections on slavery and his concern for the lessons that Europeans would need to learn from Africans, as he claims that the latter were more advanced in practicing "justice, mercy, and truth"![19]

Wesley's sense that true religion does not go from the greatest to the least but from the least to the greatest[20] is yet another example of his willingness to learn from those under pressure who are pushed to the margins by dominant power. Not surprisingly, in his "Plain Account of Christian Perfection" he reminds those going on to perfection that they need to continue to be taught not only by people like himself "but by the weakest Preacher in London; yea, by all men," adding that it is a mistake "to imagine none can teach you, but those who are themselves saved from sin."[21]

In all of this, deep solidarity and works of mercy as means of grace are closely related to works of piety, and putting them together makes all the difference: those who engage and are engaged at this level are enabled to read the Bible with fresh eyes, to pray in more profound ways, and to deepen their experience of God and others in Holy Communion. Those who read the Bible in this context will realize the deep concerns for poverty and justice. How is it possible that so many Christians, Methodists included, overlook thousands of passages that speak

19 John Wesley, "Thoughts upon Slavery," *Works,* 11:64-65.

20 In a journal entry of May 21, 1764, Wesley stated that "religion must not go from the greatest to the least, or the power would appear to be of men." Wesley, *Works,* 3:178. Almost two decades later, Wesley expressed this insight the other way around in a sermon in the year 1783: "'They shall all know *me,*' saith the Lord, not from the greatest to the least (this is that wisdom of the world which is foolishness with God) but 'from the least to the greatest,' that the praise may not be of men, but of God." John Wesley, "The General Spread of the Gospel," in *Bicentennial Edition,* 2:494. The biblical references are to Heb. 8:11 and Rom. 2:29.

21 John Wesley, "A Plain Account of Christian Perfection," *Works,* 11:428. For an intriguing story Wesley tells about the liberative effect of listening to a strange woman whom others declare "mad," see "A Remarkable Providence," *Works,* 11:497–98.

about this?[22] Those who pray in this broader framework are less likely to engage in pious monologues. And in this context, the Methodist tradition of the Open Table makes sense, because it defeats the narcissism that is so pervasive when it comes to this sacrament. According to the liturgy, invited are all "who earnestly repent of their sin and seek to live in peace with one another": the Open Table is not a free-for-all but a place of restoring relationship and engaging in deep solidarity. Holy Communion is where it all comes together and where relationships are developed further: between the self, others, and God, informed by readings of the Bible and prayer. In sum, deep solidarity with others and with God is what discipleship is all about—in opening up to others we learn to open up to God, and in opening up to God we learn to open up to others.

Reform and Revolution

Where does that leave charitable giving and advocacy? If charity and advocacy lead to reform, deep solidarity leads to revolution: nothing will be the same, as all relationships are being transformed—those with others, those with God, and—last but not least—even those with the environment.[23] Understood in the context of the means of grace, works of solidarity (mercy) serve as the strongest possible clue that we are talking not about works righteousness but about the exact opposite: works of solidarity (mercy) are done not in order to earn salvation but in order to open ourselves up to God's grace and to become more open to God and to others.

The same is true for works of piety: reading the Bible, praying, and participating in Holy Communion are done not to earn salvation but to open ourselves up to God's grace and to become open to God and to

22 See the impressive editions of the *Poverty and Justice Bible*, where all of these passages are highlighted.

23 Several of the chapters in this volume emphasize the relationship with the environment, in particular the one by Upolu Lumā Vaai.

others. The point is that transformation is put in motion by the grace of God under pressure, the experience of which moves us into action together. Charity and advocacy, by contrast, often leave us with the assumption that transformation is put in motion by what we do.

Deep solidarity places us in relation with those we intend to support and with God, helping us realize that we share some important concerns (recall that solidarity grows out of experiences of pressure that point to some common experience of sin and evil), making us ready for deeper experiences of grace under pressure that might surprise us. Transformation happens not because we are optimistic about our ability to reform the pressures we encounter; transformation happens because we learn to take the pressures more seriously than we ever have and, for this reason, invite God's revolution and join it.

The ever-growing pressures of our time and the increasing need for charity and advocacy can help make us more aware of the seriousness of the situation and that there can be no easy fix. The challenge of Anselm of Canterbury still stands: "You have not yet considered the gravity of sin."[24] As we begin to address the gravity of sin and the pressures we experience together, our differences do not fade away but can be put to use more productively. In the process, our relationship with God deepens—experiencing and valuing differences among humans can open us up to experiencing and valuing the difference of God—and even our engagement with the works of piety is transformed.

The point of deep solidarity and of works of solidarity (mercy) as means of grace is, therefore, not to make everyone look alike. The point of deep solidarity is to realize the pressures that are upon us and then to employ our differences—as well as our limited privileges—for the common good. Those who endure the greatest pressures in their own bodies are the guides in our quest for grace under pressure and the profound nature of sin: they help us become aware of how the pressures of our time destroy lives and communities, how they increasingly affect

24 Anselm of Canterbury, *Cur Deus Homo*, trans. Janet Fairweather, in *Anselm of Canterbury: The Major Works*, ed. Brian Davies and G. R. Evans (Oxford: Oxford University Press, 1998), 305.

all of us, and they put us on a search for the root causes. Wesley seems to have known this instinctively, as would most people who dare to pay attention to the pressures of life.

As we deepen our relationships and our sense of solidarity, those of us who enjoy more privileges can put these privileges to use for meaningful transformation: rather than supporting systemic racism, white people can use their white privilege in solidarity with racial minorities to bring down oppressive structures. In the process, white privilege is being deconstructed. The same is true for male privilege, ethnic privilege, and even for heterosexual privilege. The early Methodists, following the General Rules of avoiding "softness and needless self-indulgence" and "being in every kind merciful after their power," must have understood some of these dynamics.[25]

Deep solidarity reminds us that the traumatic pressures experienced by racial, ethnic, and sexual minorities are somehow linked to the pressures experienced by the majority of the 99 percent, who are no longer in control in the world of neoliberal capitalism, even if this has not sunk in yet for many people. What if the divisions of racism and sexism, for example, serve mostly the elites (the proverbial 1 percent)? When white and black, male and female, gay and straight, Latinx and Anglo working people are played off against each other, who ultimately benefits? Deep solidarity helps us resist this fracturing that is a result of sin, linked closely to the divide-and-conquer tactics used by the power brokers, and deep solidarity allows us to form new relationships that create both the power and the energy to make real differences.

Grace under pressure is experienced most profoundly, therefore, when we know what we are up against, realizing that we need each other because even middle-class people are not as powerful as they are led to believe, and start deepening our relationships with each other and with God. Working in solidarity with our sisters, brothers, siblings, communities, and the environment calls for taking sides. Even the 1 percent are not excluded; they are invited to take the side of those

25 The General Rules of the Methodist Church, http://www.umc.org/en/content/the-general-rules-of-the-methodist-church, accessed July 24, 2018.

who are struggling in the midst of the most severe pressures of life.[26] If our Abrahamic religious traditions are right, God does so as well.

Concluding Remarks: Revival

When all is said and done, Christians know that revival is the work of God. That is, of course, the point of the means of grace as well: works of piety and works of solidarity (mercy) are not effective in and of themselves but get whatever power they have from a relationship with God. This is what we are calling grace.

Of the three models dealing with the pressures of life—charity, advocacy, and deep solidarity—it is deep solidarity that displays the greatest potential to experience God at work in grace under pressure. Deep solidarity reminds us that we are not in control, that we need others and God in order to understand sin and deepen our experience of grace, and that we can do nothing without working together with others and with God.

As a result, what might spark the next revival is not the social engagement and the activism of a few privileged Methodist Christians, and neither is it the triumphalist spirituality of the mountaintops that is preached by so many today. What might spark the next revival—and what will ultimately lead beyond reform to revolution—is engaging in deep solidarity with others and with God, experiencing grace under pressure in places where we least expect it.

---

26 Everyone knows, of course, that "rich people have problems, too." But we need to start with the pressures that endanger the survival of millions of people and the earth and work our way up from there. Grace under pressure demands no less.

PART THREE

Ecological Perspectives

CHAPTER SIX

Sustaining the Planetary Household

Methodist Contributions to an Ecological Economy

Timothy R. Eberhart

Keywords: global household, biodiversity, *Oikonomia*, commons

Introduction

The context in which Methodist Christians seek to be faithful to the God of Jesus Christ and the Holy Spirit is one that will be increasingly marked by a variety of biospheric changes threatening both human and more-than-human life. Methodist ecumenical, interfaith, and public engagements worldwide will include addressing and responding to such environmentally related crises as climate refugeeism, flood, fire, drought, famine, and profound political-economic instability. As environmental, climate, and ecological justice advocacy grows, both as a worldwide movement and as a complex set of perspectives and practices adopted by diverse religious, governmental, and nongovernmental individuals and groups, global Methodist communions will be faced with countless opportunities to engage, partner with, and learn from ecologically minded Christians and non-Christians. In particular, the enormous but essential task of transitioning toward an economic system that sustains rather than degrades biospheric life in its rich and manifold forms raises a key question for we the people called Methodists: what do we have to contribute, in collaboration with others, to what Thomas Berry called the "great work" of integrating all human activities into the rhythms and limits of Earth's dynamic systems?[1]

Following a review of the dominant socio-ecological crises facing humanity today, this chapter will set forth a broad outline of an ecological economic vision for the global household (*oikos*) that draws upon a diverse set of figures representative of the egalitarian, life-sustaining, and justice-oriented contributions of the Methodist, Holiness, and Pietist traditions.

Contextual Considerations: The Age of Intersecting Crises

The present age is one defined by multiple interconnected crises, including those especially related to climate change, energy depletion, ecological degradation, and economic inequality.[2] Each of these crises, taken alone, presents an enormous challenge to the modern industrial economy and the global network of human societies, institutions, and material practices bound up in its functioning. Together they constitute a potentially ominous future defined by unprecedented social upheaval and human suffering.

Climate Change

The basic scientific explanation of the processes contributing to global warming or climate change is relatively easy to understand, although the potential effects are still difficult to grasp. With the burning of

1 Thomas Berry, *The Great Work: Our Way into the Future* (New York: Broadway Books, 2000).

2 See, for example, *Sparking a Worldwide Energy Revolution: Social Struggles in the Transition*, ed. Kolya Abramsky (Edinburgh: AK, 2010).

fossil fuels like coal, oil, and natural gas, carbon released from combustion mixes with oxygen to form carbon dioxide, which ascends into the atmosphere with other greenhouse gases like methane and nitrous oxide to create a kind of insulating blanket, trapping heat from the sun radiating off the earth that would have otherwise escaped back into space. Climatologist James Hansen notes that over the last ten thousand years, the number of parts of carbon dioxide per million (ppm) in the atmosphere has hovered around 275. This amount has produced temperatures warm enough to melt the ice sheets from the centers of our continents, allowing us to grow grain, but cold enough for mountain glaciers to provide yearly drinking water. Every aspect of our creaturely life and the human civilizations that have developed over this time have adapted to those climatic conditions. Since the dawn of the Industrial Revolution, that amount number has risen steadily each year. Back in 2008, Hansen and his colleagues concluded that 350 is the number we could reach before we do irreparable harm to the biosphere.[3] As of the spring of 2020, the global daily average was at 418.12.[4]

The resultant increase in average global temperatures of a degree and a half Fahrenheit is causing the climatic changes that are becoming everyday news around the world—a spike in the number and severity of hurricanes, the melting of the ice caps far more quickly than scientists predicted even a decade ago, severe droughts combined with increased lightning strikes causing mega-fires across entire regions, unprecedented torrents of rain and hail, super blizzards followed by massive spring floods, the acidification of oceans disrupting the marine food chain, and more. According to the scientific community, if individuals, communities, and governments do not act swiftly to reduce

3 J. Hansen, Mki. Sato, P. Kharecha, D. Beerling, R. Berner, V. Masson-Delmotte, M. Pagani, M. Raymo, D. L. Royer, and J. C. Zachos, "Target Atmospheric CO2: Where Should Humanity Aim?" *Open Atmospheric Science Journal* 2 (2008): 217–31. doi:10.2174/1874282300802010217.

4 See "Trends in Atmospheric Carbon Dioxide," Earth System Research Laboratories, Global Monitoring Laboratory. https://www.esrl.noaa.gov/gmd/ccgg/trends/monthly.html, accessed on May 25, 2020.

carbon emissions, we will likely trigger a series of negative feedback loops (e.g., releasing methane trapped in the frozen tundras) that could raise global temperatures enough by century's end to cause the extinction of most life-forms on Earth.[5] "Climate is our planet's largest, most important, and most vulnerable interlocking system," Sally McFague writes. "All of the other issues we care about cannot occur unless our planet is healthy. . . . Climate change, quite simply, is the issue of the twenty-first century."[6]

Energy Depletion

The modern industrial economy is utterly dependent upon the concentrated power released through the burning of fossil fuels. Nearly every action of modern Western life relies upon processes powered by oil, coal, and/or natural gas. Formed over millions of years through the decomposition of dead plants and animals buried, pressurized, and heated deep beneath the earth's crust, fossil fuels represent a one-time source of compact, transportable, and dense energy. As with any finite, nonrenewable resource, the depletion of fossil fuels is inevitable at some point. Over the last few decades, a growing body of literature has begun to examine the implications of "peak oil"—the point at which the rate of global oil production reaches its highest point. No one disputes that the sharp increase in the global rate of oil production, of extraction and refinement, since the start of the Industrial Revolution has powered enormous economic and population growth worldwide.

The disagreement among energy experts relates to the exact timing of when aggregate global oil production will reach its apex. Regardless of the precise timeline, once peak hits, the slope downward is not as gradual as the upward slope, because as the supply of oil reaches its highest point, demand for oil will continue sharply to increase as

5 See Bill McKibben, *Earth: Making a Life on a Tough New Planet* (New York: St. Martin's Griffin, 2011).

6 Sally McFague, *A New Climate for Theology: God, the World, and Global Warming* (Minneapolis: Fortress, 2008), 14–15.

the non-Western world follows the path of economic growth through industrialization. The peak in oil production does not signify "running out of oil," therefore, but it does mean the end of cheap oil, as market leverage shifts from consumption/demand to supply. It also signals a transition from the extraction of readily accessible oil to expensive, hard-to-reach oil, like that drilled a mile beneath the surface of the Gulf Coast waters or the dirty oil extracted from the tar sands in Canada.

These practices are bound up with heightened costs and risks and most often provide far less net energy than more conventional methods. Whether peak oil has occurred or remains years off, the fact remains that "declines in the amount of affordable energy available to society threaten to create major environmental, economic, and social impacts as the twenty-first century progresses."[7]

Ecological Degradation

The destructive effects of modern production and consumption patterns upon the health of the earth and its manifold creatures and interlocking bio-systems are innumerable. Whether one points to the pollution of air and water, deforestation, species extinction, the loss of arable farmland, or the disruption of ecosystems, it is clear that the heavily consumptive lifestyles promoted and required by a global economy dependent upon endless growth are calamitous to the whole and constitutive parts of the biosphere. The ongoing loss of the planet's biodiversity is emblematic. In an essay titled "Peak Nature?" Stephanie Mills writes that "it is estimated that between fifty million and one hundred million different kinds of microbes, fungi, plants, and animals make up" our planetary home, each inhabiting a unique place within various ecosystem households.[8]

---

7 Daniel Lerch, "Six Foundations for Building Community Resilience," in *The Community Resilience Reader: Essential Resources for an Era of Upheaval*, ed. Daniel Lerch (Washington, DC: Island, 2017), 11.

8 Stephanie Mills, "Peak Nature?" in *The Post Carbon Reader: Managing The 21st Century's Sustainability Crises*, ed. Richard Heinberg and Daniel Lerch (Healdsburg, CA: Watershed Media, 2010), 97.

Without biodiversity, human life could not exist. To give just one example, Mills says that "about 70 percent of Earth's flowering plants depend on insect pollination," including "most of the crop species that provide about a third of the goods and beverages we consume."[9] At present, many of the world's pollinators are threatened, including the all-important honeybee, due to modern industrial farming methods. A syndrome called colony collapse disorder began threatening beehives around the world in 2006, and the problem continues to worsen. The honeybee is one species. Mills quotes the United Nations' Millennium Ecosystem Assessment, which states that "the structure and function of the world's ecosystems changed more rapidly in the second half of the twentieth century than at any time in human history," resulting in a "substantial and largely irreversible loss in the diversity of life on Earth."[10]

Economic Inequality

The extractive logics and operations that characterize industrial capitalism are similarly bound up with the exploitation and degradation of workers and communities. Within the United States, real wages for the bottom 70 percent of laborers have remained unchanged since 1979, which has led to more people working an increasing number of hours and assuming greater levels of household debt. Inversely, the wealth gained from the unceasing and ever-expanding production and consumption of goods and services is concentrated in an increasingly smaller percentage of the population.

The top .01 percent in the United States now owns more than 40 percent of the country's entire wealth, which is more than the bottom 90 percent combined. Racial and gender inequities compound these trends, such that Black Americans make just around 55 percent of what is made by white Americans, and women earn on average about 20

9 Ibid., 99.
10 Ibid., 106.

percent less than men.[11] Relatedly, the concentration of wealth among an elite few undermines the social foundations of a democratic society, as the global corporate elite use their economic power to determine public policy, leading to the widespread privatization of public goods, the reduction of social programs aimed at the common welfare, and the elimination of any worker and environmental regulations that might negatively impact financial profits. Taken together, these dynamics point to "a future characterized by hereditary aristocracy and racial economic apartheid."[12]

The interconnected crises of climate change, resource depletion, ecological degradation, and economic inequality constitute the defining macro issues of our time. The warning issued almost thirty years ago by the Union of Concerned Scientists sounds with even greater urgency today:

> We the undersigned, senior members of the world's leading scientific community, hereby warn all humanity of what lies ahead. A great change in our stewardship of the earth and the life on it is required if vast human misery is to be avoided and our global home on this planet is not to be irretrievably mutilated.[13]

Home Economics for the Planetary Household

Precisely because the environmental, economic, and sociopolitical crises of our time stem from the logic and material processes of the modern global economy, the chief human task of advancing "a great change in our stewardship of the earth" requires a profound change in the nature and structure of our global economic life together. As environmental ethicist Cynthia D. Moe-Lobeda says, the world's peoples are

---

11 Sarah Byrnes and Chuck Collins, "The Equity Crisis: The True Costs of Extractive Capitalism," in Lerch, *Community Resilience Reader*, 97–98.

12 Ibid., 98.

13 "1992 World Scientists' Warning to Humanity," Union of Concerned Scientists website, http://www.ucsusa.org/about/1992-world-scientists.html.

impelled today "to reconfigure the economic dimension of life, to reorient it toward building ecologically sustainable and socially just ways of living on planet Earth." For people of faith, in particular, she suggests that "the role of religion in the twenty-first century includes offering the gifts of religious traditions to this pan-human and interfaith task."[14]

Before offering what I believe to be important contributions to this great work from traditions associated with the global Methodist movement, contributions compatible with key perspectives and practices of the modern environmental movement, it will be helpful to identify briefly my primary assumptions about the meaning and purpose of economic life.

Oikonomia

The English word *economy* comes from two Greek words: *oikos* and *nomos. Oikos* refers to a household or home. *Nomos* refers to laws or rules. In its most basic sense, then, economy simply means the household rules, the management of the household. *Oikos* is also the root word for *ecology* (*oikos* and *logos*), or the study of our planetary household, and ecumenical (*oikos* and *menikos*), which refers to the inhabited/shared worldwide household. How we address the interconnected issues raised by these three *oikic* words—economy and ecology in the global household (*oikoumene*)—will determine the kind of future we can expect for human beings and myriad other life-forms.

Oikonomia, or the management of the household, is the most ancient meaning of *economy.* Aristotle, for example, distinguished *oikonomia* from *chrematistics.* The one, *oikonomia,* he described as the management of the material resources of the household for the benefit of all its members over the long run. For Aristotle, this is the true form of economy. The other, *chrematistics*, he said, relates to the manipulation

14 Cynthia D. Moe-Lobeda, *Resisting Structural Evil: Love as Ecological-Economic Vocation* (Minneapolis: Fortress, 2013), xix.

of property and wealth so as to maximize short-term monetary gain for the individual owner. Aristotle viewed such activities with disdain.[15]

The modern meaning of economics follows this second path. Modern economics, which is just over two hundred years old, is focused on the rules or managerial techniques needed to maximize monetary wealth for the individual actor as quickly as possible. Modern economics is the art of individual money-making. Those committed to the upbuilding of an ecological economics for the flourishing of all God's creation would do well to look to the older meaning of *oikonomia*. Here the most basic question of economy is not "how can I, a self-interested individual, make as much money as possible?" but rather "how shall we order the household for the benefit of all?" or "how shall we make a home?"

Agrarian author, farmer, and environmental activist Wendell Berry has long called for the reconstitution of economic life based in an affirmation of the immediate and symbolic importance of homemaking. In his 2012 Jefferson Lecture in Humanities given after receiving the highest honor given by the National Endowment for the Humanities, Berry said:

> I am nominating economy for an equal standing among the arts and humanities. . . . I mean, not economics, but economy, the making of the human household upon the earth: the arts of adapting kindly the many human households to the earth's many ecosystems and human neighborhoods. This is the economy that the most public and influential economists never talk about, the economy that is the primary vocation and responsibility of every one of us.[16]

---

15 Aristotle, *The Politics* (London: Penguin Books, 1981), book 1.

16 Wendell Berry, quoted in Scott Carlson, "We Are All Implicated: Wendell Berry Laments a Disconnection from Community and the Land," *Chronicle of Higher Education*, April 23, 2012, http://chronicle.com/article/In-Jefferson-Lecture-Wendell/131648/.

Setting the Table

At the center of nearly every household is the table. The table or the meal gathering is the center, both material and symbolic, around which most other household activities are organized—and this is true of a family meal, a seminar table in a university, a corporate boardroom, or almost any of the world's religious traditions. It is around a table that our most basic patterns of household life together are determined. Here, at table, I would argue, we encounter the most basic questions of economy:

1. *Who gets to sit at the table?* This is about who has access to the means of life and who does not.
2. *What kind of bonds are formed around the table?* This is about the nature of our socio-ecological relations.
3. *Do the elements served nourish the body?* This is about the sustainment and health of our earthly life or lack thereof.
4. *How are the seats arranged?* This is about how power is structured.
5. *In whose name is the meal blessed?* This is about ultimate aims and allegiance.

These are all questions of economy, and the way in which they are answered determines how our households are ordered, whether at the personal, congregational, institutional, national, or even global level. So what are we to contribute as Methodist Christians? If we are to participate in shaping the economy to come—locally, nationally, globally—what might we contribute from the perspective of our unique history, faith, and experience? What do we believe to be right and good and even joyful about how households are to be managed, about how life together around the table is to be shared?

The scriptures are clear that the God of Israel, of Jesus Christ and the Holy Spirit, is deeply invested in the questions of how households are managed, of homemaking, of table practices. From the house of Pharaoh to the manna economy to the Torah instructions concerning the poor (e.g., gleanings; usury prohibition; justice for aliens, widows, and orphans; Jubilee) to the prophetic criticisms of the monarchs to

Jesus's announcement of the inauguration of the divine economy, God is revealed as the economist working to create the conditions of home for the whole of creation.[17]

As we Methodist Christians participate with non-Christians in the emergence of an ecological economy for the well-being of all, it is possible, I believe, to identify areas of convergence between certain perspectives and practices of the modern environmental movement and a range of distinctive affirmations found within our Methodist, Holiness, and Pietist roots. The emphases or characteristics that tie these later traditions together are many, including a criticism of theologies detached from everyday life, an insistence upon the inseparability of doctrine and ethics, a preferential focus upon the poor and oppressed, an affirmation of the priesthood of all believers, a commitment to communicating in the language of common life, an avowal that the Christian life is life together in community, and the offering of concrete proposals for both ecclesial and social reformation in each new age. At the heart of these emphases is the shared theological perspective that God's love constitutes the essence of God's being and work, that God calls and empowers us to be holy as God is holy in the whole of life, and that the primary locus and aim of holy living is loving communion with others.[18] With these theological and moral distinctives in mind, I propose that in the household of God that Jesus proclaims and incarnates, centered in particular around a peculiar set of table practices, the five basic questions of economy can and ought to be answered by us Methodists in the following ways.

---

17 See M. Douglas Meeks, *God the Economist: The Doctrine of God and Political Economy* (Minneapolis: Fortress, 1989).

18 The unifying doctrinal emphasis of these traditions of the doctrine of Christian perfection or entire sanctification has materialized historically through active participation in abolitionism; the inclusion of women in teaching and preaching roles; ministries with and for the poor and oppressed; radical critiques of money, privilege, and existing social structures; consistent emphases upon peace and nonviolence; and affirmations of simplicity of lifestyle. See Donald W. Dayton, "The Holiness Churches: A Significant Ethical Tradition," *Christian Century*, February 26, 1975, 197–201.

God's Economy for the Whole Creation[19]

1. *Who gets to sit at the table?*

The God of Jesus Christ invites everyone. All are given free access to the basic means of life, beginning especially with the poor, the vulnerable, and the excluded. There is more than enough for all. We see this in the feeding of the multitude stories, where Jesus hosts a meal, much like the manna meal, in which "all ate and were filled" (Matt. 14:20, NRSV). Theologically, the claim is that in Jesus Christ the divine holiness is revealed as *gracious love* for all. As the fourteenth-century mystic John Ruusbroec affirmed, "Christ went out to all in common in his love, his teaching, and his admonitions; in the way he tenderly consoled and generously gave. . . . He gave himself completely to all in common, does so still, and will do so for all eternity, [for] he was sent to earth for the common benefit of all."[20] Faithfully responding to the divine summons to "be holy as I am holy," then, means following after Jesus in the way of gracious love for all in common. The table commandment issued in one of the banquet parables is simply this: "Go therefore and invite everyone you find" (Matt. 22:9).

To be faithful to this command—to follow Jesus today—entails criticizing any arrangement of the household, locally or globally, that excludes people from access to the basic means of life. Proponents of capitalism have long portrayed the global economy as if it were an open

19 For an extensive treatment of these themes, see my book *Rooted and Grounded in Love: Holy Communion for the Whole Creation* (Eugene, OR: Pickwick, 2017), from which the following section is adapted and revised. Used by permission of Wipf and Stock Publishers. www.wipfandstock.com.

20 John Ruusbroec, *The Spiritual Espousals and Other Works* (New York: Paulist, 1985), 106–7. Ruusbroec's writings and model of communal life were the primary source of inspiration for Geert Grote, the founder of the Brothers and Sisters of the Common Life (Devotio Moderna). One of the earliest members of the Devotio Moderna, as well as the chief biographer of Grote, was Thomas à Kempis, whose understanding of holy living was a significant influence on John Wesley.

web of partnerships accessible to all willing to play by its rules and succeed on its terms. The claim is that, through the supposedly peaceful coordination of individual persons, unfettered markets inherently produce prosperity for all who freely participate in the pursuit of self-interested gain. The reality, however, is that as the logics and operations of capitalism have spread worldwide, more and more peoples have been expelled, often violently, from direct access to the most basic means of life, livelihood, and daily sustenance.

Many in the environmental movement point to the enclosure of lands as emblematic. Indian activist Vandana Shiva traces the origins of modern capitalism to the enclosure of lands that, beginning in sixteenth-century England, began the uniquely modern process of excluding the majority of humans from direct access to food, water, and other sources to sustain life.[21] In almost all societies prior to capitalism, she argues, the multitude of people subsisted through immediate relationships to the earth and its fruits. Worldwide, the enclosing of the commons and dispossession of the multitudes has continuously created "surplus" or "disposable" people. Ultimately, the only remaining option for those made landless has been to migrate to urban centers, where they sell their labor to those who own the means of production and work under exploitative conditions. This same pattern has followed the spread of free-market capitalism around the world.

> The industrial system has . . . in virtually every area of the globe, "enclosed" farmland, forcing subsistence peasants off the land, so that it can be used for growing high-priced export crops rather than diverse crops for local populations. . . . Removed from their land and means of survival, the new "landless" then flock to the newly industrialized cities where

---

21 See Vandana Shiva, *Earth Democracy: Justice, Sustainability, and Peace* (Cambridge, MA: South End, 2005), 19–27.

they quickly become a class of urban poor competing for low-paying jobs and doomed to long-term hunger or starvation.[22]

In God's economy, by contrast, all are given access to the necessary means for life. God's gracious love for all in common is especially manifest in the inclusive nature of Jesus's table practices. In fact, throughout the Gospels, Jesus particularly seeks out and invites those who have been excluded from the goods of table fellowship. We who claim to follow Jesus's radically inclusive love are called to work for a public household in which the efficiencies of the private marketplace do not overtake the common goods of an inclusive society that works for all and is accessible to all.

One of the ways individuals and communities can participate in Jesus's holy way of gracious love is by engaging in efforts to bring about policy and legal changes at the national and international levels to ensure that all people have immediate access to the productive potentialities of the earth. One of the founders of the modern environmental movement in North America, Liberty Hyde Bailey (1858–1954), recognized the fundamental linkages between a genuinely democratic society, proper care for the land, and the universal access of all citizens to what he called the "holy earth." Precisely because the earth, as Bailey saw it, is a "gift" from God and "is not selfish" but "is open and free to all" and "invites everywhere," we should "begin to understand the awful sin of partitioning the earth by force."[23] Bailey's vision for the United States was that "every person should have the right and the privilege to a personal use of some part of the earth."[24]

While advocating for larger structural reforms, Christians can and ought to support initiatives in their local communities as well to

22 Andrew Kimbrell, tntroduction to *The Fatal Harvest Reader: The Tragedy of Industrial Agriculture*, ed. Andrew Kimbrell (Washington, DC: Island, 2002), 7.

23 Liberty Hyde Bailey, *The Holy Earth: Toward a New Environmental Ethic* (Mineola, NY: Dover, 2009), 31, 34.

24 Ibid., 35.

increase what Nobel Prize–winning economist Elinor Ostrum calls "common-pool resources,"[25] through efforts like community gardens or land trusts that preserve woodlands or native prairies for public use and enjoyment. As agro-economist Jack Ralph Kloppenburg says, "To begin the global task to which we are called, we need some particular place to begin, some particular place to stand, some particular place in which to initiate the small, reformist changes that we can only hope may some day become radically transformative."[26] In so doing, by participating in the gracious nature of God's love manifest in Jesus Christ for the well-being of all in a particular place—via church lands, parking lots, and other properties owned by denominations, congregations, or individual members—Christians thereby prepare the ground for the possibilities of broader economic reforms to come. We Methodist Christians might view such local efforts, knit together through various connectional structures, as an ecological expression of Wesley's charge to "spread scriptural holiness across the land."[27]

2. What bonds are formed around the table?

The Holy Spirit joins everyone together in bonds of loving fellowship. The nature of the socio-ecological relations that are formed around the table of God's economy are mutually life-giving, for the Spirit gathers diverse others together in bonds of genuine communion. From a Wesleyan-Methodist perspective, the theological affirmation is that the divine holiness is present with us in the Holy Spirit as *convivial love.* Faithfully responding to God's invitation to participate in the divine holiness, then, means abiding in the spiritual bonds of love with, for, and among others.

---

25 Elinor Ostrom, *Governing the Commons: The Evolution of Institutions for Collective Action* (New York: Cambridge University Press, 1990), 183–84.

26 Jack Ralph Kloppenburg, "Coming into the Foodshed," *Agriculture and Human Values* 13, no. 3 (1996): 41.

27 John Wesley, "The 'Large' Minutes, A and B (1753, 1763)," in *The Bicentennial Edition of the Works of John Wesley*, vol. 10, *The Methodist Societies: The Minutes of Conference*, ed. Henry D. Rack (Nashville: Abingdon, 2011), 845.

We become holy as God is holy by "sharing in the Spirit" (Phil. 2:1), who is present as the source of harmonious life together. For this reason, love for God and love for others are ultimately inseparable, for when we love one another we are sharing in the love of God, which is present to us in the Holy Spirit. The call to holiness, moreover, is not restricted to certain spheres or relationships, for the will of God is for our *entire* sanctification (1 Thess. 5:23). This is a "going on to perfection," as Wesley described it—an ever-deepening alignment with the love of God in the Holy Spirit infusing all the relationships of life. For "by perfection," he writes, "I mean the humble, gentle, patient love of God and our neighbor, ruling *all* our tempers, words, and actions."[28] The table command here, as Paul says, is "whether you eat or drink, or whatever you do . . . let *all* that you do be done in love" (1 Cor. 10:31, 16:14).

To be faithful to what the Spirit is doing in the world today—to abide in the Holy Spirit—therefore means first of all criticizing economic structures that are based in the fragmentation of long-standing relationships and communities. Proponents of modern capitalism regularly depict the global free-market economy as if it were a near-perfect mechanism for interweaving the world's peoples and natural elements into a web of harmonious partnership. The claim is that through the coordination of society's self-interested individuals, free markets naturally bring about social equilibrium in general and personal well-being for individual actors. The reality, however, is that while the exchange of commodities through global markets has bound more and more people, places, and materials together, social and ecological bonds are being disrupted and fractured.

In this regard, the environmental movement has focused particular attention upon the destructive effects of modern industrial agriculture on native ecosystems. From an ecological perspective, a healthy ecosystem is a natural area within which an astoundingly rich communion of life-forms intermix, comingle, and cohabitate in complex ways to

28 John Wesley, *A Plain Account of Christian Perfection* (New York: Epworth, 1952), 112.

sustain the diversity of life-forms—both the parts and the whole—in that place. Among the chief strategies of industrial agriculture is the isolation and manipulation of particular plant varieties or animal traits in order to increase production and thus financial profit.

Driven by the logics of efficiency, economy of scale, and the profit motive, modern agro-economic practices have replaced small and midsize diversified farms with massive monocrop or livestock operations that focus on just one part of the food economy. Modern industrial agriculture's primary focus on increasing global food production is dependent on technologies such as large-scale machinery, synthetic nitrogen fertilizers, pesticides, and herbicides, all of which are contributing to many of today's ecological crises. Over the past forty years, these technologies are responsible for a 30 percent loss in the world's farmable land and the release of more than 25 percent of the world's carbon emissions, 60 percent of all methane gas emissions, and 80 percent of nitrous oxide emissions, all of which are major contributors to atmospheric climate change.[29] Profit-driven monocrop agriculture is also a primary culprit of biodiversity loss worldwide.

In God's economy, centered around the love feast of convivial relationship, all the members of the body are woven together in life-sustaining harmony. This is the central theological and moral affirmation for Paul amid the various food controversies in the early church. Whatever the situation, "do not seek your own advantage," he concludes, "but that of the other" (1 Cor. 10:24), for God's holiness is present not in any particular food or drink but within the "righteousness and peace and joy in the Holy Spirit" (Rom. 14:17). To abide today in the convivial love of the Holy Spirit through relational bonds of peace must therefore include supporting methods of production and consumption through which human and more-than-human participants are gathered together in ways that foster social and ecological health. This means looking to sustainable agricultural methods, regenerative farming practices, permaculture techniques, and/or indigenous food

29 Kimbrell, introduction, 6–36.

traditions, all of which focus upon increasing biodiversity, intermixing and rotating a variety of plants and animals, and fostering as many beneficial relationships as possible. Those "going on to perfection," as Wesley says, will embrace what Wendell Berry describes as "an elaborate understanding of charity,"[30] which extends the love of neighbor into the multitude of relationships gathered up in and through the food we produce and consume. By shifting emphasis away from increasing the yields of a singular crop for commodity exchange and toward a broader emphasis on nurturing convivial relationships among a diversity of participants, those who practice agro-ecology are more closely aligned, we can affirm, with the healing energies of God's convivial love. Similarly, Christians who focus upon the health and well-being of others, both human and nonhuman, through the food decisions they make and the agro-economic system they support, both personally and politically, are seeking to abide more faithfully in the divine holiness seeking to join all together in harmony and peace.

3. Do the elements served nourish the body?

God the Father/Mother nourishes our bodies with the bread of life and the cup of salvation. God's intention is for the healthful sustainment of the whole of creation. In the last supper he shares with his disciples, Jesus says, "This is my body, this is my blood" (Matt. 26:26, 28). God is given to us in the form of life-giving bread that sustains our bodies to do the work of God. "My food," Jesus says, "is to do the will of the one who sent me and to perfect his work" (John 4:34). The theological claim here is that the divine holiness from the Father/Mother is offered to us as *enfleshed love,* which nourishes our earthly life. The Father/Mother offers his/her love to us in bodily form, so that we who are his/her creatures can receive and be sustained by it.

As Radical Pietist Johann Christoph Blumhardt writes, the work of God is not, as most think, oriented toward heaven. "It is the heavenly

30 Wendell Berry, *The Gift of Good Land* (San Francisco: North Point, 1981), 273.

coming to reality upon earth. . . . It is earthly because it is a concern that the situation on earth become good and righteous, and that God's name be hallowed on earth, that his kingdom come on earth and his will be done right here on earth. The earth is to manifest eternal life."[31] Faithfully responding to God's invitation to participate in divine holiness, then, means worshipping the Father/Mother by nurturing the bodily well-being of creaturely existence. The movement of the Father/Mother's love is from the creator toward the earthly creation, which means we properly "worship the Father in spirit and in truth" (John 4:23–24) by tending to the flourishing of the earth and all God's creatures. The table commandment here is to "present your bodies as a living sacrifice, holy and acceptable to God, which is your spiritual worship" (Rom. 12:1).

To be faithful to the God who nourishes our bodies with life-giving food means first of all criticizing economic structures that prioritize the generation of abstract, financial wealth over the real wealth of healthy human bodies and vibrant ecosystems. Those who champion the spread of capitalism worldwide contend that the coordination of individual self-interest through unfettered markets is one of the most powerful generators of wealth in human history. The reality, however, is that the ongoing growth of financial wealth, increasingly concentrated among fewer and fewer beneficiaries, is directly related to the ongoing degradation of bodily and planetary well-being.

One of the central errors of capitalist economic logic, according to many environmental critics, is the denial of the fundamental primacy of land and nature in the production and sale of commodities for financial profit. Instead of seeing the elements and systems of the earth as categorically different than human-made products exchanged through the

31 Johann Christoph Blumhardt, "The Kingdom of God Is for Earth," in *Thy Kingdom Come: A Blumhardt Reader*, ed. Vernard Eller (Grand Rapids, MI: Eerdmans, 1980), 3. For an introduction to the place of Blumhardt and his son in the Holiness/Pietist tradition, see Frank D. Macchia's text *Spirituality and Social Liberation: The Message of the Blumhardts in the Light of Wurttemberg Pietism* (Metuchen, NJ: Scarecrow, 1993).

marketplace, the logics of capitalist production place value upon the soil, air, water, and other natural elements only to the extent they can be converted into profit. The natural world, however, is not just one among a set of interchangeable goods but rather is the basic precondition of all human activity, including economic activities. "Nature is the world's dominant producer," as Vandana Shiva writes. "The production of humus by forests, the regeneration of water resources, the natural evolution of genetic products, the creation of fertile soil from eroding rock. . . . Human production shrinks to insignificance in comparison with nature."[32]

One of the principal ways that human and ecological costs are hidden through the extractivist operations of capitalism is through the externalization of costs, or what Wendell Berry calls the "false accounting" of a money-oriented economy.[33] While owners of production are able to extract a near endless supply of goods from the biosphere and then privatize them through various forms of enclosure, they simultaneously unload many of the social and environmental impacts back into the commons. Because producers are rarely required to internalize such costs into their operations, many of the worst human and ecological effects of the global economy go unaccounted for in the final prices of the goods and services we consume.

A related error is a naive belief in limitless economic growth. Proponents of unfettered capitalism continue to argue that there is no limit to the global economy's capacity to expand, both by extending the number of those enjoying first-world consumptive lifestyles and by continually improving standards of living with an endless supply of commodity goods. But "it does not require more than a simple act of insight," as E. F. Schumacher asserts, "to realize that infinite growth of material consumption in a finite world is an impossibility."[34] The

---

32 Shiva, *Earth Democracy*, 16.

33 See Wendell Berry, "The Idea of a Local Economy," in Norman Wirzba, ed., *The Art of the Commonplace: The Agrarian Essays of Wendell Berry* (Washington, DC: Counterpoint, 2002).

34 E. F. Schumacher, *Small Is Beautiful* (New York: Harper and Row, 1973), 114.

dependence of modern industrial societies on nonrenewable resources, in particular, such as coal, oil, and natural gas, represents a clear limit to economic growth.

Alternatively, in the divine economy, participants are invited to "taste and see" that the Lord and the whole of earthly creation are good. Worshipping the Father/Mother in economic life—and thus participating more fully in the divine holiness—means finding ways of integrating economic activities into the limits and needs of the biosphere. Those who begin with the recognition that our human economy exists within clear planetary boundaries will strive toward what Herman Daly calls "steady-state" economies. In such economic systems, the combined input of material resources and energy into the economy and the total output of waste materials and heat do not exceed the regenerative and absorptive capacities of the earth's many systems. A truly sustainable economy, as Daly says, requires mechanisms that internalize rather than externalize the full costs of production, distribution, and consumption to ensure we do not extract more from the earth's "natural capital" than we put back.[35]

In an integrated economy centered on the sustainable production and consumption of goods for the sake of creaturely well-being, qualitative value is as important an indicator of economic health as quantitative value. In an economy oriented toward the sustenance of the earth and all its creatures, the key question therefore is not simply, How can we produce, market, and sell the greatest number of commodities for the highest possible financial return? Instead, questions related to the qualitative properties of products and the manner in which they were produced become equally if not more significant.

Such an approach is fundamentally congruent with the logic Wesley articulates in his sermon "The Use of Money." Wesley's first instruction to "earn all you can," for example, is qualified by the provision that "we ought not to gain money at the expense of life," which he specifies as any work which is harmful to one's body or mind

35 See Herman Daly, "Economics in a Full World," *Scientific American*, September 2005, 100–107.

(i.e., working around arsenic, engaging in sinful trade) or is hurtful to another (i.e., land enclosures, usury, the production of unhealthy goods). The second instruction, to "save all you can," includes wasting no part of one's resources "in curiously adorning your houses in superfluous or expensive furniture; in costly pictures, painting, gilding, books; in elegant (rather than useful) gardens," because all wealth beyond what is necessary for sustaining one's life and the life of one's family belongs to the poor. Finally, after earning and saving all they can, Methodists, he argues, ought to "give all you can" for the good of those who suffer in need.

> In the hands of his children it is food for the hungry, drink for the thirsty, raiment for the naked. It gives to the traveler and the stranger where to lay his head. By it we may supply the place of an husband to the widow, and of a father to the fatherless; we may be a defense for the oppressed, a means of health to the sick, of ease to them that are in pain.[36]

For Wesley the primary purpose of economic life, therefore, is not the increase of short-term, abstract financial value but rather the material sustainment and bodily health of creaturely life. For Methodist Christians today, that must entail engaging in the production, distribution, and consumption of real goods and services that foster the flourishing of human and more-than-human others as a means of faithfully worshipping the Father/Mother in economic life.

4. *How are the seats arranged?*

The God who is Triune arranges dinner guests as coequal companions. Those who participate in this meal are mutual servants of one another, each one assisting the other for the sake of the common good. In this arrangement of the household, power is shared cooperatively

36 John Wesley, "The Use of Money," in *John Wesley's Sermons: An Anthology*, ed. Albert C. Outler and Richard P. Heitzenrater (Nashville: Abingdon, 1991), 348–57.

and coequally. Here we recall Jesus's response to his disciples who are arguing over who will sit next to him at the messianic banquet: "The Kings of the Gentiles lord it over them . . . but not so with you, rather the greatest among you must become like the youngest, and the leader like one who serves" (Luke 22:25–26). From a Holiness-Methodist perspective, the claim is that in the Holy Trinity, the divine holiness is shared as *mutual love*, which flows out to the creation that we might love our neighbors as ourselves in upbuilding the common good of all. "Life in God means gathering," as Eberhard Arnold affirms. The will of God is that we be knit together in an "organic unity composed of many members who are committed to one another and support one another."[37] Faithfully responding to God's invitation to "be holy as I am holy," therefore, means conforming to the triune God by joining with and being for our neighbors in the formation of concrete communities of mutual, cooperative service. The table commandment is this: "Each of us must please our neighbor for the good purpose of building up the neighbor" (Rom. 15:2).

To be faithful to the God who is triune means first of all criticizing any arrangement of the public household in which economic wealth and political power are concentrated in the hands of an elite few. One of the recurring claims made by proponents of free-market capitalism is that the global market economy operates with no centralized organization. The reality is that, while the global economy does operate through a worldwide network of partnerships, the ongoing consolidation of corporate and state power is simultaneously consolidating economic and political control among fewer and fewer actors. Naomi Klein describes this process as "corporatism,"[38] Michael Nollert as the "emergence of transnational economic elites,"[39] and Michael Hardt and Antonio

37 Eberhard Arnold, quoted in *God's Revolution: The Witness of Eberhard Arnold*, ed. John Howard Yoder (New York: Paulist, 1984), 111, 113.

38 See Naomi Klein, *No Logo* (New York: St. Martin's, 2000).

39 See Michael Nollert, "Transnational Corporate Ties: A Synopsis of Theories and Empirical Findings," *Journal of World-Systems Research* 11, no. 2 (2005): 289–314.

Negri as "empire" or "biopower."[40] Similarly, Wendell Berry has written that "the centralization of our economy" and "the gathering of the productive property and power into fewer and fewer hands" is leading to the "consequent destruction, everywhere, of the local economies of household, neighborhood, and community."[41]

At the heart of concerns about centralized power is a critique of the modern corporation. Environmental economist David C. Korten has argued that modern corporations have replaced the state and the church as "*the* dominant governance institutions on the planet."[42] Korten traces the rise of the modern corporation to fifteenth- and sixteenth-century England and Holland, where landowners who had amassed agricultural wealth from the privatization and enclosure of common lands were seeking to reinvest their capital in new ventures for further profit. Unlike the productive enterprises they replaced, in which small groups of people who knew one other operated businesses they would have co-owned, the new corporate form of joint stock companies allowed for the sale of stock to strangers by corporate managers. This new form, Korten writes, combined two ideas:

> the sale of shares in public markets and the protection of owners from personal liability for the corporation's obligations. These two features made it possible to amass virtually unlimited financial capital within a single firm, assured the continuity of the firm beyond the death of its founders, and absolved owners of personal liability for the firm's losses or misdeeds.[43]

In the United States, the extension of constitutional rights for individual persons to private corporations has allowed corporations to claim

---

40 See Michael Hardt and Antonio Negri, *Empire* (Cambridge, MA: Harvard University Press, 2000).

41 Wendell Berry, *What Are People For?* (New York: North Point, 1990), 128.

42 David C. Korten, *The Post-corporate World: Life after Capitalism* (West Hartford, CT: Kumarian, 1988), 60.

43 David C. Korten, *The Great Turning: From Empire to Earth Community* (Bloomfield, CT: Kumarian, 2006), 131.

full citizenship rights while being exempted from many liabilities and responsibilities. As a legal "person," the modern limited liability, joint stock corporation in the United States has gained tremendous power to shape contemporary social and political life. Through the spread of corporate power worldwide through neocolonialism, developmentalist policies, structural adjustment loans, and now free-trade agreements, and by way of ongoing mergers and acquisitions, corporations have gained tremendous power over the structures of the global political economy, resulting in the amassment of the world's financial resources and political power by fewer and fewer actors.

In God's economy, by contrast, power is shared equally. All share and enjoy the goods of creation through cooperative relationships. Jesus warns his disciples to "beware of the yeast"—the hierarchical table practices—of the religious elites and rulers of imperial power (Mark 8:15). Instead they are to follow their host in assuming the role of mutual service. "For who is greater, the one who reclines at table, or the one who serves? Is it not the one who reclines at table? But I am among you as one who serves" (Luke 22:27). Those seeking to gather in conformity to the mutual service of the triune God incarnate in Jesus are called today, I would argue, to participate in cooperative modes of economic life together.

Among the many ways they might do so, including advocating for and supporting the transition beyond capitalism toward democratically socialist forms of political economy, I will point here to local efforts to share in what Korten calls "local-living economies."[44] In a local-living economy, the focus of economic activity is centered upon the locally sufficient production of goods and services for regional consumption, with only the surplus being used for external trade. Whatever cannot be produced locally is sourced from community-oriented companies and small farms located in other economic bioregions. By keeping wealth circulating within a local region, political and economic power

---

44 David C. Korten, *Change the Story, Change the Future: A Living Economy for a Living Earth* (Oakland, CA: Berrett-Koehler, 2015).

is thus allowed to concentrate in democratically governed townships, neighborhoods, or any variety of small collectivist organizations.

A local-living economy resembling the divine fellowship of coequal persons is constituted by a diverse collective of local companies of various sizes committed to a set of cooperative, egalitarian business practices. One of the key foundations of such companies is the sharing of ownership and workplace governance among employees. In cooperative employee ownership structures, those who create the products and resultant wealth enjoy equal shares of the generated wealth, thereby preventing unequal balances of power and wealth between ownership and labor, managers, and staff. Employees also participate democratically in the many decisions of the workplace, such that even as there are diversity of roles and tasks to accomplish, each member is able to influence the daily operations and overall direction of the workplace.

Companies that are committed to not only financial profit but also community development and ecological sustainability also seek out opportunities to contribute to the people, area institutions, and local landscapes of which they are members. In the present context of the unjust and undemocratic control of corporations over more and more aspects of our daily lives, Christians seeking to participate in the mutual love of the triune God should be working to build up and support cooperative enterprises committed to egalitarian, democratic, and community-oriented business practices.

5. *In whose name is the meal blessed?*

The God of Jesus and the Holy Spirit grants permission for the feast of life to begin. The one to whom Christians commit our ultimate allegiance is the host of the household who announces that the universal reign of loving justice is already at hand. Already in this present age, the power of God's eternal holiness breaks forth as *creative love*, which frees us to partake in fruitful ventures of a new life together. Here we remember that the primary image of the coming kingdom of God in the scriptures is that of a messianic feast, and that in Jesus's own ministry, it was his festive and disruptive table practices that enfleshed his proclamation that "the kingdom of God has come near" (Mark 1:15).

A world that would otherwise be bound to an eternal perpetuation of that which has always been is continuously opened up to new possibilities by the creativity of God's sovereign love. "A new reality appears, a reality that is opposed to the world's history," as Christoph Friedrich Blumhardt affirms. "God's kingdom is the revelation of the divine life here on earth, the birth of new hearts, new minds, new feelings, new possibilities."[45] Or, to speak with Wesley, salvation "is not something at a distance" but "is a present thing, a blessing which, through the free mercy of God, ye are now in possession of."[46] Faithfully responding to God's invitation to participate now in the divine holiness, then, means accepting the liberty we are given to "obey God rather than any human authority" (Acts 5:29). For we know that "our citizenship is in heaven" (Phil. 3:21) and that the inbreaking of God's sovereign love into this world authorizes us to "stand firm" and "not submit again to a yoke of slavery" (Gal. 5:1). Christian freedom is thus "the creative passion for the possible," as Jürgen Moltmann says, manifest in the implementation of "new, unguessed-at possibilities" in the world.[47] The table commandment is this: "New wine must be put into fresh wineskins" (Luke 5:38).

To begin now the banquet feast of God's just economy means first of all criticizing forms of household arrangements marked by imperial colonization. Proponents of the global spread of capitalism argue that

---

45 Christoph Friedrich Blumhardt, *Action in Waiting* (Farmington, PA: Plough, 1998), 18–20.

46 John Wesley, "The Scripture Way of Salvation," in *John Wesley's Sermons*, 372.

47 Jürgen Moltmann, *The Spirit of Life: A Universal Affirmation* (Minneapolis: Fortress, 1992), 119. As early as 1975, Moltmann was directly turning to "experiences of the ancient congregational churches," such as "the Waldensian congregations, the Mennonites and the Moravian Brethren." Moltmann, *The Church in the Power of the Spirit* (Minneapolis: Fortress, 1993), xiv. In his work in pneumatology in recent decades, Moltmann has come to draw more heavily on German Pietism, early Methodism, and medieval mysticism.

free markets are the most effective and democratic way of organizing the distribution of goods and services throughout a society. Whereas governments are overburdened by bureaucratic inefficiencies and corruption, they claim, and whereas centralized control stifles individual freedom, open markets are supposed to provide the conditions in which the innovation and creativity of free individuals automatically generates economic growth through the so-called invisible hand of the market. The reality, however, is that the worldwide opening of more and more spheres of existence to the logic of free markets has allowed for the expansion of corporate dominion over more and more aspects of social and ecological life. The reality is that capital is the god to whom we are truly bowed down.

Vandana Shiva describes the progressive invasion of the profit motive into ever-new spheres across three major waves. The first took place, she argues, during the five hundred years of European colonization of the Americas, Africa, Asia, and Australia. The second, postcolonial wave has occurred over the past five decades through the Western imposition of "developmentalism" on so-called undeveloped nations. The third wave, she says, is taking place today through patents, genetic engineering, and intellectual property rights. "The land, the forests, the rivers, the oceans, and the atmosphere have all been colonized, eroded, and polluted." In pursuit of new spaces to invade, privatize, and exploit for financial profit, she says, "the colonies have now been extended to the interior spaces, the 'genetic codes' of life-forms from microbes and plants to animals, including humans."[48]

Over the last several decades, the corporate drive to possess private ownership over more and more aspects of the economy has led to the colonization of the inner space of living organisms. With science having advanced in its capacity to understand and manipulate life at the genetic level, to commercialize biotechnical research, and to extend property rights to genetically modified life-forms, corporate interests have been able to commoditize the material elements of life itself.

48 Vandana Shiva, *Biopiracy: The Plunder of Nature and Knowledge* (Boston: South End, 1997), 4–5.

Corporate ownership of living organisms at the molecular and genetic levels has been made possible by a series of legal decisions allowing the patenting of "novel" life-forms. As a result, "virtually all living organisms in the United States, including human genetic material, became patentable subject matter, just like any other industrial invention."[49] Jack Ralph Kloppenburg concurs:

> In what is frequently likened to a nineteenth-century style "land grab," vast tracts of the genescape and its products—DNA sequences, exons, introns, individual mutations, expressed sequence tags, single nucleotide polymorphisms, proteins, protein folds, parts of plants, whole organisms, whole classes of organism—are being appropriated via patents.[50]

In the economy of God, centered around the messianic feast, persons are liberated from the principalities and powers of this age to serve God at home, at work, in the public square and marketplace. Those of us striving to obey the table host's invitation to begin the feast now ought to withdraw our cooperation with economic systems of colonial domination while participating together in creative modes of life that support the growth of a new economic order. At the very beginnings of our modern political economy—nearly five hundred years before transnational corporate entities would claim exclusive ownership over plant and animal genes—Thomas Müntzer openly declared that the source of "all usury, theft, and robbery" in society are the self-interested lords and princes "who take all creatures for their private property." For "the fish in the water, the birds in the air, the animals of the earth," he warned, "must all be their property (Is. 5:8)."[51]

---

49 Hope J. Shand, "Intellectual Property: Enhancing Corporate Monopoly and Bioserfdom," in Kimbrell, *Fatal Harvest Reader,* 243.

50 Jack Ralph Kloppenburg, *First the Seed: The Political Economy of Plant Biotechnology* (Madison: University of Wisconsin Press, 2004), 324.

51 Thomas Müntzer, "A Highly Provoked Defense," in *The Radical Reformation,* ed. Michael Baylor (New York: Cambridge University Press, 1991), 81.

Although the modern age has seen Christian movements claim emancipation from various forms of repressive control, there have been few who have successfully declared freedom from the economic forces overruling nearly every aspect of contemporary life. In working toward a new economic order, in which love for neighbor guides our economic practices and decisions, Christians affirm their allegiance to the God whose transcendent freedom from the world is manifest in the power to bring about a new reality in and for the world.

There is perhaps no better starting point for those seeking to support the emergence of a new economic reality in our time than with the food economy. For the inbreaking of God's kingdom into this present age forces a decision about who or what truly governs our daily lives. That decision is clearly concentrated in two very different meal gatherings: the capitalist-driven agribusiness meal marked by imperial conquest and corporate dominion and the joyous banquet feast born of God's perfect love for the whole of creation. The reality is that a few private corporations possess ubiquitous command over nearly every aspect of the production and distribution of most foods that we eat.

As a result, unless we are willing to seek out and support the few alternative food sources that presently exist, as Marion Nestle says, "we support the current food system every time we eat a meal."[52] Nevertheless, having been liberated to begin the kingdom feast already here and now, Christians are free to support existing food alternatives, however small and imperfect, while helping to create models and systems that are even more closely aligned with God's reign of loving justice. Because the food economy is so foundational to any economic system, the eruption of new, more charitable and sustainable ways of producing and distributing food has the potential to redirect the entire global economic order. According to Shiva, small-scale, direct responses are "necessary in periods of dictatorship and totalitarian rule because large-scale structures and processes are controlled by the dominant power."

---

52 Marion Nestle, *Food Politics: How the Food Industry Influences Nutrition and Health* (Berkeley: University of California Press, 2003), 374.

In particular, everyday essentials such as "our seeds, our rivers, our daily food are sites for reclaiming economic, political, and cultural freedoms because these are the very sites of the expanding corporate empire over life."[53]

By participating directly in grassroots movements for justice and in struggles to transform our global economy, including the ways we gather up and share the fruits of the earth in table fellowship, Christians participate faithfully in the divine holiness that is laboring to redeem all things through creative love.

Conclusion

In an age of climate change, resource depletion, ecological degradation, and economic injustice, Methodist Christians worldwide are joined with the peoples of the earth in a common task to envision and work toward new models of economic life together—or new arrangements of the household—that nurture rather than harm our common planetary home. As I have attempted to demonstrate, Holiness-Wesleyan understandings of the holistic love of God—marked by gracious inclusion, convivial harmony, enfleshed integration, mutual cooperation, and creative freedom—are congruent with key affirmations and practices found in the modern environmental movement. In giving witness to God's life-sustaining and just economy through missional engagement for the sake of the world God so loves, including especially with ecologically minded non-Christians, the people called Methodists, I believe, will find grateful and interested partners ready to receive and share with us in the great work of our time.

The invitation is simply this: "Come for everything is prepared" (Luke 14:17). Because the host invites everyone with gracious love, the earth is a commons, accessible to all. Because the Spirit of the feast joins all together in convivial love, the exchange of goods and services fosters social and ecological health. Because the bread and cup nourish

53 Shiva, *Earth Democracy*, 183.

everybody as love enfleshed, all our productive activities are integrated into the rhythms and needs of the earth. Because guests are assembled in mutual love, neighborly partnerships are arranged in cooperative communities. And because the head of the banquet blesses its commencement with creative love, all are set free to begin now the new economy in which both people and planet enjoy the present blessings of abundant life.

CHAPTER **SEVEN**

Methodist Environmentalism in African Context

Retrieving John Wesley's Ethic of Care and Environmental Protection

R. Simangaliso Kumalo and Kisitu Gyaviira

Keywords: Methodism, environment, Wesleyan environmental ethic, environmental protection, South Africa

Introduction

Protection for the environment has preoccupied reflections of ecologists, environmentalists, historians, and many others, as well as theologians across faith traditions in recent decades.[1]

1 In this chapter, *nature, creation, cosmos, created world, physical world,* and *environment* are terms used synonymously to refer to the environment. Generally, this means the physical environment, even though while discussing the environment from within the African worldview it is recognized that this notion includes not only the physical but also the spiritual realms. We take note that the term *environmentalism* is contentious especially when discussing issues of ecological theology given its possible association with environmentalists who may not necessarily believe in God. We, however, use this term because it provides a wider platform in analyzing and critiquing human

One of the key concerns has been the urgent call to recognize the ecological crisis as a reality in the present time. The changing weather patterns, rising temperatures, reduction in water levels, and loss of natural diversity are some of the known indicators of the ecological crisis experienced today. Attempts to respond to the issue of ecological crisis have been characterized in part by a search for its cause. For instance, human activity and the role of theology (including Methodist theology) have been questioned for their contribution. While some studies have argued that human activities such as industrialization, science, and technology have greatly increased the rate of environmental pollution, other studies have blamed Abrahamic religions for seemingly encouraging human domination of nature. This being the case, it is imperative to note that Christianity has also contributed voices of resistance to environmental destruction.

Christian leaders from various denominations of Protestant, Orthodox, Roman Catholic, and Methodist churches have taken leading roles in emphasizing the need to preserve the environment. Theologies that deal with environmental justice have been developed, and calls to heal the natural environment have intensified. This does not mean, however, that the world has come out of the imminent dangers due to the destruction of the environment. Disasters related to environmental destruction, which we continue to experience today, suggest need for further action. This chapter refers to the state of environmental degradation in South Africa and the role of the Methodist Church in the country. Through the Wesleyan ethic of environmental protection, the chapter analyzes the various approaches used by the church in the promotion of environmental awareness and justice and discusses the extent of their contribution. The chapter argues that the Wesleyan ethic of environmental protection is relevant to the African context in the

---

actions as far as environmental protection is concerned irrespective of religious affiliations or traditions. The term is also accommodative in discussing African worldviews and spiritualities on environmental protection to which we make reference in this chapter.

struggle toward environmental protection and can be further enriched by the environmentally friendly African cultural values.

Contextual Considerations: Conceptualizing the Term *Environment*

The term *environment* is not limited to one definition or understanding. It is widely understood from various perspectives, and at times limitations are drawn regarding what constitutes the environment. Popularly, *environment* has been used to mean nature, even though this in itself raises other questions such as: what is nature? Nature has been understood in terms of what is visible to the human eye, such as landscapes, vegetation, bodies of water, and other living organisms. In other ways, the term has been explained from an anthropocentric point of view, limiting the meaning to the extent of service to human needs. For instance Paul H. Selman speaks of environment as that which "refers to the physical and biological systems which provide our [human] basic life support, and which contribute to our psychological well-being."[2] Schools of knowledge informed by sciences, such as cosmology, metaphysics, environmental science, theology, and astronomy, have gone further to explain that environment is far more sophisticated and includes much more than what is naturally visible to the human eye. In this chapter, we shall understand the environment to mean the natural world in which human persons live while recognizing the role and complexity of relationships involved within.[3] This is also integrated with the African concept of interconnectedness known as *ubuntu* to further understand the concept of environment especially from the African perspective.

2 Paul H. Selman, *Environmental Planning: The Conservation and Development of Biophysical Resources,* 2nd ed. (London: Thousand Oaks, 2000), 1.

3 Michael Allaby and Chris Park, *A Dictionary of Environment and Conservation* (Oxford: Oxford University Press, 2013), 114.

African worldviews speak of the interconnectedness between nature, or the physical world, and human beings in reference to how humans understand the meaning of environment. Environment is a community not only of the human persons but also of all that nature consists of. The concept of community, as Harvey Sindima points out, "suggests bondedness; it refers to the act of sharing and living in communion and communication with each other and with nature."[4] Sindima's observation is right in the sense that while many human societies recognize the value of living in relation with each other, they also perceive nature as a vital support for human existence. Nature provides food, medicine, food for livestock, and protection, and it is through nature that human societies also communicate with the spiritual world and seek blessings and guidance. In some communities, for instance, forests, rivers, and lakes have the same names as human persons or deities. In Uganda, Lake Victoria is locally known as Nalubaale, also a human surname. Some rivers are also identified with names associated with humans, such as the Mayanja and the Ssezibwa. The naming conventions suggest that nature and persons can be described as "one, woven by creation into one texture or fabric of life, a fabric or web characterized by an interdependence between all creatures."[5] Interdependence therefore teaches people to live in community not only with one another but also with the rest of creation. John Kaoma has observed that

> Ecologically, the African dependence on the world of plant, insect, and animal species for remedies to social and psychological problems seems to confirm the unity and involvement of all living species in human life. Humanity may claim to

4 Harvey Sindima, "Community of Life: Ecological Theology in African Perspective," Religion Online. https://www.religion-online.org/article/community-of-life-ecological-theology-in-african-perspective/. Accessed December 18, 2019.

5 Ibid.

> be the crown of creation, yet without the power resident in nature, *umuntu* (human being) is highly vulnerable.[6]

We can infer therefore that from the African perspective, the understanding of nature or environment is associated with harmonious living in which the physical world and the spiritual world are intimately connected in a mutual relationship, so much so that abuse of this connection is taboo or an abomination.

Even though inhabitants of the physical environment ought to harmoniously relate with each other, this has not been the case. In their work "Sustainability and Viability," Neil Stewart and Gerald Lewis consider human beings to have had an overwhelming negative impact on the ecosystem in the last two hundred years. The scholars argue that "it is almost not possible to think of a natural world. . . . There are now quite clear signs that the biosphere's ecological systems are showing signs of distress."[7] It is therefore imperative to note that while in the past several hundred years the world has been fascinated with epochs of enlightenment and industrial revolution, especially in the seventeenth and eighteenth centuries, in the twenty-first century we are faced with environmental degradation that has led the world and its inhabitants into what can be described as an ecological crisis. To speak of an ecological crisis is to recognize the visible lack of harmony in nature and the deteriorating abilities of organisms' relationships to ensure each other's survival.

In contemplating the root cause of environmental degradation and a possible way forward, environmentalists have identified human activities and human antienvironmental epistemologies as key contributors to ecological crisis. Our present dialogue on the negative impact of

---

6 Kapya J. Kaoma, *God's Family, God's Earth: Christian Ecological Ethics of Ubuntu* (Zomba, Malawi: Kachere Series, 2014), 99.

7 Neil Stewart and Gerald Lewis, "Sustainability and Viability," in *Systems for Sustainability: People, Organizations, and Environments*, ed. Frank A. Stowell, Ray L. Ison, Rosalind Armson, Jacky Holloway, Sue Jackson, and Steve McRobb (New York: Plenum, 1997), 97.

human activities and epistemologies over the earth's environment is not merely a phenomenon of recent years. From the middle of the twentieth century, the world was exposed to such impacts through works such as Rachel Carson's *Silent Spring* in 1962 and Lynn White Jr.'s groundbreaking essay "The Historical Roots of Our Ecological Crisis" in 1967. Carson cited and critiqued human population growth and advancing technology as threats to the survival of various ecosystems, including human life.

Unsettled by the anthropocentric interpretation of biblical texts, White challenged Christianity. He argued that the anthropocentric worldview, which put nonhuman creatures at the mercy of humans, was detrimental to the environment, as it uses the Bible to authorize human dominion over the rest of creation. For White, unless Christianity embraces the kinship of humanity with the rest of nature as depicted in St. Francis of Assisi's model, the world would continue to be prone to ecological crises.[8]

Having highlighted a conceptual understanding of the term *environment* with close attention to its perception from the African context, we now turn to the Methodist Church in South Africa.

Methodist Church and the Environmental Challenges in South Africa

The Methodist Church community is one of the largest religious communities in South Africa under the umbrella group of the Methodist Church of Southern Africa (MCSA). The MCSA extends territorial presence into neighboring countries such as Mozambique, Lesotho, Swaziland, Botswana, and Namibia. In South Africa, the Methodist Church is influential in areas of social transformation and the development of society, as it has been over the years, including during the Apartheid era. As Wessel Bentley notes, "Methodism is well known in

8 Randy L. Maddox, "Anticipating the New Creation: Wesleyan Foundations for Holistic Mission," *Asbury Journal* 62, no. 1 (2007): 51.

the South African context, especially in the rural areas. It is known for its progressive role in building communities and facilitating processes, which on the one hand exposed injustice, but also served as instruments of reconciliation."[9] In spite of its long-standing mission and legacy in areas of social transformation and development, the Methodist Church faces a critical challenge when it comes to the issues of environmental protection.

In the area of environmental protection, very few South African Methodists have taken keen interest in promoting environmental justice and awareness of the ecological crisis the world faces today. Those few who speak about this problem seek to draw inspiration from Wesleyan environmental theology and from African cultural values on environmental protection. Despite these attempts, the MCSA continues to struggle in developing a Wesleyan environmental ethic of preservation. There is virtually no project on environmental awareness by the denomination. P. Malinga Nomthandaso further emphasizes that the Methodist church in southern Africa still exhibits "failure to take environmental issues seriously, [and] the inability to connect soul, soil and society."[10]

While the denomination does not have a well-coordinated strategy for environmental awareness, some of its congregations are involved in such projects as planting trees, water harvesting, and food gardens. Such interventions are few and coordinated without denominational knowledge or funding. As a result, these projects make little tangible impact in solving the problem. This is unfortunate, because as an African church, the MCSA has both religious and cultural resources from which it can draw knowledge for environmental care. But whether the church fails to demonstrate enough concern for the environment or

---

9 Wessel Bentley, "Methodism and Transformation in South Africa: 20 Years of Constitutional Democracy," *HTS Theological Studies* 70, no. 1 (2014): 4. Available at http://hdl.handle.net/10500/14431.

10 P. Malinga Nomthandaso, "The Presiding Bishop-Elect's Report," *2020 Yearbook: The Methodist Church of Southern Africa* (2020): 22. https://methodist.org.za/wp-content/uploads/2020/03/Yearbook-2020-003-final-2.pdf.

seems to be unaware of the imminent environmental problems and their effects, the problem is not erased. It remains a reality in the South African context and at the global level.

The Reality of Environmental Challenges

Nature's deterioration and accelerated levels of species extinction are increasingly being noted at a global level. Statistics indicate that since about four decades ago, the world has experienced increased gas emissions, doubling its previous levels to the extent that the average global temperature has been rising. The cause of most of these problems has been pinned on human activities or on human failure to address the problem of environmental degradation and its consequences.[11] From a global perspective, environmentally concerned institutions continue raising awareness, especially for the need to control global temperatures and limit gas emissions so as to increase possible adaptability to adverse effects of climate change.

From a South African perspective, the subject of environmental degradation remains complex. Section 24 of the 1996 South African Constitution states that

> everyone has the right to an environment that is not harmful to their health or well-being; and to have the environment protected, for the benefit of present and future generations, through reasonable legislative and other measures that prevent pollution and ecological degradation; promote conservation; and secure ecologically sustainable development and use of

11 "UN Report: Nature's Dangerous Decline 'Unprecedented'; Species Extinction Rates 'Accelerating,'" Sustainable Developmental Goals, May 6, 2019. https://www.un.org/sustainabledevelopment/blog/2019/05/nature-decline-unprecedented-report/.

> natural resources while promoting justifiable economic and social development.[12]

Despite the above constitutional guarantee, the country faces significant cases of environmental threats. These include but are not limited to increased air and water pollution, especially from the mining industry; global warming and climate variability and their effects; desertification; land degradation; and waste and litter mismanagement.[13] These environmental risks cast significant doubts as to how committed the country is to its environmental protection advocacy. The roles of stakeholders, including members of the civil society, politicians, nongovernmental organizations, and religious bodies, are called into question as to what extent these bodies contribute to environmental protection. Could the escalating effects of environmental degradation in South Africa be explained by a tendency of various organizations of influence to undermine certain environmentally friendly knowledge or by their failure to perceive and protect the environment as a necessary companion of the human race?

The highlighted state of affairs in regard to the environmental challenges cannot leave the Methodist Church in South Africa indifferent. This is because the church seems to have certain resources from which it can draw inspiration and tools to engage in active environmental protection interventions. It can be argued that the Wesleyan environmental ethic and African environmental spiritualities present inspiration that may be of relevance to the Methodist Church to address environmental challenges in the African context.

---

12 "South Africa's Constitution of 1996 with Amendments through 2012," Constitute Project. https://www.constituteproject.org/constitution/South_Africa_2012.pdf?lang=en. Accessed December 12, 2019.

13 M. B. Kwesi Darkoh, "An Overview of Environmental Issues in Southern Africa," *African Journal of Ecology* 47, suppl. 1 (2009): 93–98. https://doi.org/10.1111/j.1365-2028.2008.01054.x.

A Brief Overview of the Wesleyan Environmental Ethic

Today many theologians agree to the proposition that protecting the environment is a moral good and the obligation of human beings. It not only correlates with a responsibility with which they have been endowed by the creator but also is a means of ensuring their survival and that of generations to come.

Stretching back to John Wesley's time, the theological and ethical significance of the physical world was compromised by ideas inspired by Neoplatonism. Central to Neoplatonism is the role of hierarchy in describing, understanding, and categorizing forms of emanations. Under this mode of thought, layers of emanations are not significantly equal in their representations of reality, and the reality of existence is defined by thought and intellect but not matter. At the time of Wesley, the world was greatly under the wave of the Enlightenment and the rise of capitalism, which drew much influence from Neoplatonism. We know now that these forces have led to enormous environmental degradation. However, during Wesley's time, the possibilities did not cause much alarm. In fact, works of eighteenth-century theologians such as William Derham, who argued in favor of anthropocentrism to the disadvantage of nature, received little or no theological challenge at the time. Derham insisted that "we can if need be, ransack the whole globe, . . . penetrate into the bowels of the earth, descend to the bottom of the deep, travel to the farthest regions of this world, to acquire wealth, to increase our knowledge, or even only to please our eye or fancy."[14]

Like Derham, Robert Barclay, an influential Quaker theologian of the seventeenth century, believed in the supremacy of the human person over the rest of creation, just as God is supreme over the human person. Barclay taught that "whatever thing the Creation affords, is for

---

14 William Derham, *Physico-theology, or, A Demonstration of the Being and Attributes of God from His Works of Creation* (London: Innys, 1713; rpt., New York: Arno, 1977).

the use of man, and the moderate use of them is lawful."[15] The Puritan vision of nature and the human person during the sixteenth and seventeenth centuries followed a similar trajectory. In the Puritan vision of nature, it seemed proper for the "Puritan elect to dominate, subdue Nature, and vanquish wilderness."[16] This is because nature was viewed to possess a lesser degree of perfection and to occupy the lowest level in the hierarchy of creation.

No doubt creation under an anthropocentric view was no more than at the service of the human person's desires. Humanity alone, believed to be endowed with intelligence and rationality, crowned itself chief over all creation to the extent that it could do with the rest of the created order as it pleased. These views, backed by an anthropocentric Christian background, meant that the created order continued to be desacralized and secularized with no spiritual significance by both Christians and non-Christians alike. This does not mean, however, that John Wesley was in agreement with this approach. As Howard Snyder states, "Wesley was not oblivious to the created order, but he seemed ambivalent about it."[17] One of the reasons why less attention was directly paid to issues of the environment is that the slave trade dominated theological discussions of the time. Attempts to discourage progression of the slave trade and showing how the practice contravened biblical teachings on love of neighbor were more pressing for theologians such as Wesley.[18] Such concerns were also intertwined with economic exploitation of the poor and an influential power of capitalism. The period especially from the

15 Quoted in Kelley Donald Brooks, "The Evolution of Quaker Theology and the Unfolding of a Distinctive Quaker Ecological Perspective in Eighteenth-Century America," *Pennsylvania History: A Journal of Mid-Atlantic Studies* 52, no. 4 (1985): 243.

16 Ibid.

17 Howard A. Snyder, *Yes in Christ: Wesleyan Reflections on Gospel, Mission and Culture*, vol. 2 (Toronto: Clements, 2011), 94.

18 Samuel Wells and Ben Quash, *Introducing Christian Ethics* (West Sussex: Wiley-Blackwell, 2010), 103.

fifteenth to the eighteenth centuries saw the accumulation of wealth and increased industrial production most often at the expense of the world's poor majority.

These issues are critical in relation to environmental concerns. Often when industries such as mining and lumbering emerge, the natural environment is compromised, as it is pressed to provide raw materials for manufacturing. Air and water sources become extensively polluted and previously forested fields are deforested, which in turn compromises the survival of species, including human persons. Studies that have attempted to establish links between environmental problems and poverty show that the poor and the most vulnerable groups such as women and children are the most affected by the repercussions of environmental degradation.[19]

Though not seen as directly championing the preservation of the environment, a Wesleyan environmental ethic can be derived indirectly from Wesley's own advocacy for the poor as demonstrated in his sermons and hymns and from themes such as the love of God and neighbor, the image of God, new creation, deliverance, and stewardship. From these themes and their theological underpinnings, we can develop principles that speak to ecological preservation and care for creation today.

One of the important themes attributed to Wesley is a love of God and neighbor that does not exclude the rest of creation. A review of Wesley's reflections reveals that many are characterized by love as both a theological and ethical category. First Corinthians 13:1–13 speaks of this love, which seems to characterize Wesley's understanding and application. In a sermon on love, Wesley's teaching goes beyond human-to-human relationships and extends its moral code to the rest of God's creatures.

---

19 Suzanne Goldenberg, "Climate Change: The Poor Will Suffer Most," *Guardian*, March 31, 2014. https://www.theguardian.com/environment/2014/mar/31/climate-change-poor-suffer-most-un-report.

> The love which our Lord requires in all his followers, is the love of God and man;—of God, for his own, and of man, for God's sake? . . .
>
> As to the measure of this love, our Lord hath clearly told us, 'Thou shalt love the Lord thy God with all thy heart.' Not that we are to love or delight in none but him. For he hath commanded us not only to love our neighbour—that is, all men—as ourselves; to desire and pursue their happiness as sincerely and steadily as our own; but also to love many of his creatures in the strictest sense—to delight in them, to enjoy them—only in such a manner and measure as we know and feel not to indispose but to prepare for the enjoyment of him. Thus, then, we are called to love God with all our heart.[20]

Wesley's emphasis on love of God, human persons, and God's creatures, argues Howard Snyder, "tended to counteract Neoplatonism," which "saw the natural order as purely instrumental for human use, and rising capitalism which saw natural resources simply as fuel for industry and commerce."[21] In Neoplatonism we can see a hierarchical measure between human persons and the rest of creation whereby the human person is at the top with an assumed authority to subjugate the rest of creatures. However, Wesley asserts that such a relationship assumes subjugation of the rest of creatures and fails to express an outward and inward holiness, which calls for concern not only for human persons but also creatures alike.

The love of God, neighbor, and creation is further grounded in the creation story, in which the creator is pleased by all creation and describes it as good (Gen. 1:31). Given the goodness of creation, it therefore appears to be intrinsically animated by the spirit of love.

---

20 John Wesley, "Sermon 139: On Love," in *Sermons on Several Occasions* (Grand Rapids, MI: Christian Classics Ethereal Library, 2003), 1235. https://www.whdl.org/john-wesleys-sermons.

21 Snyder, *Yes in Christ,* 93.

Here God loves the creation God created; the human person loves God because God is the creator, and the human person loves all the created because it was created by God. Speaking of this relationship in line with Wesley's love of God, neighbor, and all creation, Snyder notes:

> Love for God and neighbor extends to all creation. . . . We respect and guard the creation because God made it, loves it, pronounced it good, and have covenanted with it (Gen 9); and also because the well-being of our local and global neighbors depends upon environmental health.[22]

Loving the created order rather than destroying it honors God's command and the intention behind the creator describing the entire creation as good. Since in Genesis 1 God bestows goodness to the entire creation, it is therefore not limited to human persons. The rest of creation also shares in this goodness, and once human persons realize and honor this, their journey to a life of holiness is further enhanced. This is because, according to Wesley, it is not true that "a devout and holy life meant living in strict separation from the world." On the contrary, "holiness required community."[23] Wesley's usage of the concept of community without limitation and including all creation is in itself radical. In this case, the aspect of community meant that it was improper for human persons to regard the rest of creation as less valuable or insignificant. It also seems to mean that since human persons and the rest of creation are rightful members of the same community, none of the supposed members can be regarded as "merely property that can be owned, but are entities that have an independent right to exist and flourish."[24]

Living in relationship with the rest of creation also gives way to what Wesley advocated for—social holiness—which is sparked from

22 Ibid., 95.

23 Ibid.

24 "What Is Rights of Nature?" *Global Alliance for the Rights of Nature* (GARN). https://therightsofnature.org/frequently-asked-questions/. Accessed January 23, 2020.

living in mutual interconnectedness, not only among human persons but also with the rest of the creation. The theological proposition of social holiness is enhanced by the view that human persons are just as accountable for each other as they are to the rest of the creation with which they share the physical world.[25] Scholars such as Stanley J. Grenz have shared this Wesleyan spirituality. From an anthropological perspective, Grenz argues that "our identity includes being in relationship to nature, being in relationship with others, and being in relationship with God and as a consequence, being in true relationship with ourselves."[26] It would suffice to argue that this character of interdependence within creation falls under what Wesley describes as a manifestation of God's wisdom in nature. For Wesley, the physical world is beautiful and reflects the wisdom of God. In his sermon "The Wisdom of God Counsels," Wesley states:

> Now the wisdom as well as the power of God is abundantly manifested in his creation; in the formation and arrangement of all his works, in heaven above and in the earth beneath; and in adapting them all to the several ends for which they were designed: Insomuch that each of them, apart from the rest, is good; but all together are very good; all conspiring together, in one connected system, to the glory of God in the happiness of his intelligent creatures.[27]

Social justice is a controversial issue in our time even as it was in Wesley's, and environmental stewardship characterized his theological reflections in his campaign for social justice amid the economic

25 Marcus K. Kilian, *Formational Leadership: Developing Spiritual and Emotional Maturity in Toxic Leaders* (Eugene, OR: Wipf and Stock, 2018), 126–38.

26 Stanley J. Grenz, *A Primer on Postmodernism* (Grand Rapids, MI: Eerdmans, 1996), 172.

27 Wesley, "Sermon 68: The Wisdom of God Counsels," in *Sermons on Several Occasions,* 674.

exploitation and disregard of the poor of his time.[28] Social justice can be understood as a philosophy that all individuals, irrespective of who they are or where they come from and irrespective of their religious affiliations, have the right to a life of dignity. Today when the global community speaks of social justice, there are certain issues that come to mind. Among these issues are poverty, exclusion, unemployment, gender and racial inequity, and access to social well-being and justice for all. Social justice demands we pay attention to these issues and promote all necessary efforts that aim to solve any inequities, knowing that many of these issues affect the poor of society, who also happen to be the global majority.

Protection of the natural environment has much to do with social justice. What scientists and environmentalists today describe as consequences of environmental destruction, such as global warming, droughts, uncontrollable floods, and extreme storms, affect human persons and other living species in different but intersecting ways—life is destroyed, and the world increasingly becomes hostile to existence. When the environment become hostile to existence, individuals at the periphery of society—the poor, often women and children, and the old—become the immediate victims.

During Wesley's time, the world was also faced by issues of social justice, about which Wesley was concerned. Among these were issues of housing, community services, disease and suffering, slavery, low wages, corruption, and poor health care systems—what we might call the social safety net. Faced by these challenges, Wesley saw himself as an evangelist who, while "primarily concerned with the spiritual redemption of people," was also concerned with their "physical and social circumstances."[29]

---

28 H. Newton Malony, "John Wesley and Psychology," in *Psychology and Christianity Integration: Seminal Works That Shaped the Movement,* ed. Daryl H. Stevenson, Brian E. Eck, and Peter C. Hill (Batavia, IL: Christian Association for Psychological Studies, 2007), 88, 82–91.

29 Malony, "John Wesley and Psychology," 89.

Health care is one of the main channels through which Wesley emerged as a champion of social justice. The absence of a functioning health care system, which in itself caused much suffering to the poor, influenced him to research illnesses and advise the sick on which medicines to take. This was in an effort to improve the health standards of the people to whom he ministered. Even though Wesley was criticized by authorities because he was not a physician, he was nevertheless determined to minister in this way. From a biblical perspective, Wesley's concern for social justice seems to have been motivated by scriptural readings such as Isaiah 61:1, which was also quoted by Jesus: "The Spirit of the sovereign LORD is on me, because the LORD has anointed me to proclaim good news to the poor. He has sent me to bind up the brokenhearted, to proclaim freedom for the captives and release from darkness for the prisoners."

In relation to the physical environment and health of the people, Wesley believed that sickness and people's well-being were also linked to the physical environment that surrounded them and that this caused disease and suffering.[30] More important, the question of how human beings stewarded the physical goods at their disposal called for examination. This is evident in Wesley's sermon 51, "The Good Steward," in which he provides an ethical rule to enhance responsible stewardship:

> We are not at liberty to use what He [God] has lodged in our hands as we please, but as he pleases, who alone is the possessor of heaven and earth, and the Lord of every creature. We have no right to dispose of anything we have, but according to His will, seeing we are not proprietors of any of these things; they are all, as our Lord speaks, . . . *belonging to another person;* nor is anything properly *our own,* in the land of our pilgrimage.[31]

30 Ibid.

31 Wesley, "Sermon 51: The Good Steward," in *Sermons on Several Occasions,* 523–24.

Wesley shapes the ethic of environmental stewardship using Luke 16:2: "And he called him and said to him, 'What is this I hear about you? Give an accounting of your management, for you can no longer be manager.'" It could be understood in this context that to "give an account" is taking up a responsibility of action. It is also to presume that one was entrusted with certain responsibility prior to his or her being called to account. From this ethical responsibility, and in relation with the Genesis 1 creation narrative, we can argue that human beings were commissioned to take care of God's creation. Stewardship in this perspective can be understood to incorporate the creation of care practices such as water harvesting, recycling, energy conservation, and environmental protection advocacy. Following this, it becomes human beings' responsibility to avoid any form of exploitation of the environment by applying certain ethical practices that have the ability to minimize rampant exploitation of the created order.

Stewardship as we understand it today further encourages individuals to cultivate advocacy as far as ecological sustainability is concerned. Therefore, the MCSA should be teaching this kind of stewardship to its members. As already pointed out, Wesley was not directly speaking to environmental exploitation, but from his theological teachings, sermons, and hymns, we can deduce that his ethic is fundamental for the church's developing an environmental ethic of care. It can easily be seen that in many of his teachings, Wesley often challenged human actions, thoughts, and judgment, especially insofar as human beings act in disregard to God's love and the well-being of the other. Today many environmentalists agree that much of our environment has been violated mainly due to the decisions and actions that human beings have made in the past. When we look at ecological crises we experience today, human beings, in either what they have done or failed to do, cannot be exonerated as agents of ecological distortion.

In recent years, scholarship has engaged with the interplay between economic and ecological realities. As many countries continue to industrialize their economies and maximize production, limited resources necessarily threaten the abundance of "goods and services produced by nature upon which we ultimately depend."[32] Nature produces and purifies the water we drink. Nature produces and purifies the air we breathe. Nature further provides the rains and water that we need to grow our crops for food production. It is the same nature that detoxifies the environment, making soils fertile and making living organisms in soils thrive. However, the industries we run also use the same resources, such as oxygen and water, to manufacture products. In return, the by-products are released back to nature at toxic rates, weakening the ability of nature to sustain life.

Among the questions we face, as we consider the Wesleyan environmental ethic and the enormous environmental degradation of our time: How can we live an environmentally friendly life? What would a Wesleyan environmental ethic of care advocate for in this present time and context? Are there any practical values that may bring us closer to honoring a Wesleyan environmental ethic of environmental stewardship, love of God and neighbor, care for creation, social holiness, and interdependence of creation? In recognition of these questions, we propose a return to indigenous African knowledge systems of environmental protection, which have over the years been sidelined and competed against by theories of modernity and economic development. Such new knowledge, which has distanced human beings from the environment and has recognized the physical environment only as servile to humans, has led to more harm than good, especially regarding environmental sustainability.

The present and future generations of living species will not be spared by environmental calamities. However, indigenous knowledge systems and African eco-friendly cultural values see the physical environment not as a slave to humanity but as sacred and as something

32 Herman E. Daly and Joshua C. Farley, *Ecological Economics: Principles and Applications*, 2nd ed. (Washington, DC: Island, 2004), 11.

spiritual through which the ancestors communicate to the living.[33] Therefore what can African spirituality of the environment offer Christianity and humanity at large in the effort to preserve the environment from destruction? Even though not all elements of African spiritualities are compatible with Christianity, certain values can enrich the protection of nature, a project that Christian-based environmental stewardship attempts to promote.

What Can African Environmental Spirituality Offer?

One of the challenges that African Christianity faces today in creating true witnesses to combat the crisis of environmental degradation is the failure to make use of the eco-friendly indigenous knowledge systems. In this system of knowledge, the human does not intend and has no right to subdue and dominate other parts of creation but instead is obliged to promote a harmonious coexistence. This knowledge is cumulative, and it is "handed down through generations by cultural transmission, about the relationship of living beings with one another and their environment."[34] It is the type of knowledge acquired through observation and experience of the cosmos. Some scholars have attempted to describe it as either traditional or indigenous ecological knowledge.[35]

Indigenous environmental spiritualties from many African societies are not necessarily in conflict with the biblical ecological ethic

33 Yaw Adu-Gyamfi, "Indigenous Beliefs and Practices in Ecosystem Conservation: Response of the Church: Church and Environment," *Scriptura: Journal for Contextual Hermeneutics in Southern Africa* 107, no. 1 (2011): 145–55. https://doi.org/10.7833/107-0-132.

34 Fikret Berkes, "Traditional Ecological Knowledge in Perspective," in *Traditional Ecological Knowledge: Concepts and Cases*, ed. Julian T. Inglis (Ottawa: International Program on Traditional Ecological Knowledge, International Development Research Centre, 1993), 3.

35 These terms are interchangeably used here to refer to the same system of knowledge.

of stewardship, especially where these spiritualties guard against the destruction of the environment or nature and lay emphasis on human responsibility to preserve the environment. For instance, among the Akans of Ghana,

> the universe is living because the divine is actively involved in it. The universe is conceived as "neither theocratic nor anthropocentric." The human being is simply part of the whole, a responsible part and not owner of the other parts. . . . The traditional culture of Akan stresses a strong relationship with the environment. Thus the impact of the Akan view of the universe is that they have developed deep respect for nature and interact with it.[36]

From a Christian perspective, "creation has dignity because God dwells in it through His Spirit and sustains it."[37] Psalm 24 emphasizes: "The earth is the LORD's and all it holds, and the world and those who dwell in it." Romans 1:20 also suggests that God is revealed through his creation, and through it humanity can testify to the existence of God: "Ever since the creation of the world, his invisible attributes of eternal power and divinity have been able to be understood and perceived in what he has made." This therefore does not seem to be inconsistent with how the Akans of Ghana, as well as the Zulus and Tswanas of South Africa, speak of the environment, knowledge that is crucial for its protection.

Despite this, however, Christian communities sometimes seem to be less prepared to accept that African indigenous environmental spiritualties have something to offer. Nevertheless, if these spiritualties offer a framework that reflects models of ecological stewardship, could it not be time that Christianity reemphasized their recognition in sustaining coexistence of creation in local contexts? It could be argued, along with

36 Adu-Gyamfi, "Indigenous Beliefs and Practices," 146.

37 Nico Voster, *Created in the Image of God: Understanding God's Relationship with Humanity* (Eugene, OR: Pickwick, 2011), 91.

Peter F. Penner, that "we need to identify the Holy Spirit in the midst and presence of the community—explaining, teaching and leading in areas that have not been defined in scripture."[38]

In Zimbabwe, the Shona believe that the natural world provides the habitat for the spirits and sends messages from the spiritual world to the human world. The spiritual world provides guidance, punishment, and blessing to the human world. People therefore have to relate to both the natural and the spiritual world. In traditional African societies, cutting down trees in certain forests, is considered a taboo and an offense to the gods and the ancestors. Strict norms and threats, which attempt to restrict human activity in such forests are emphasized especially in so far as such activities are perceived as destroying and altering the cosmic order.[39] Human activities such as hunting, building, cultivation, food gathering, and preparation habits would be, as such, restricted in certain forests. Given the ecological crisis we face today, and the continuous destruction of the natural environment, we can perceive a moral teaching that underpins the African worldviews on the environment. For instance, restraining or keeping human activities in check is generally an attempt to preserve the environment and protect it from destruction and exploitation. It is also by extension to preserve it for the well-being of society and generations to come. This serves the theological concept of love for neighbor, as well as cultivating the virtue of responsible stewardship, both of which are very Wesleyan.

Conclusion

A debate on whether or not, or to what extent, John Wesley can be classified as an environmentalist theologian is very much alive. One of

38 Peter F. Penner, "Hermeneutics, Biblical Ethics and Christian Witness," *Journal of European Baptist Studies* 4, no. 1 (2003): 20.

39 M. Ikeke Omolovie, "The Forest in African Traditional Thought and Practice: An Ecophilosophical Discourse," *Open Journal of Philosophy* 3, no. 2 (2013): 348.

the critiques raised is an observation that Wesley neither commented directly on environmental protection nor challenged prominent schools of thought of his time. His critiques of Neoplatonism, the Enlightenment, and capitalism were overtly from the perspective of social justice. He challenged the world of his time insofar as it suppressed the poor and promoted vices such as slavery, corruption, and other abuses of human rights.

Without undermining this critique, it is also important to note that foundational principles used by environmental theologians today to defend the protection of the environment were also articulated to some extent by Wesley as he defended the poor. Such principles include seeing both humanity and the rest of creation as bearing the goodness of the creator, perceiving the human person as God's steward over creation, seeing humanity and the rest of creation as true manifestation of God's image and existence, and love of neighbor, under which humanity is called upon to rethink their actions as they affect both current and future generations. This is critical in addressing the environmental crisis today, as it will be for future generations. The question is, To what extent do our communities of faith give priority in promoting protection for the environment and in utilizing all the resources available, including the teachings from our spiritual forebears such as Wesley, toward that aim? It is also important to rediscover the role of African indigenous ecological knowledge from local contexts. This can be brought into conversation with Christian theological views with the intention of developing integrated models of environmental protection easily understood and promoted in local contexts.

CHAPTER **EIGHT**

Others Are Enjoying Life from Our Death

Eco-relational Theology and a Methodist Ecological Revolution in the Pacific

Upolu Lumā Vaai

Keywords: relationality, Pacific, Methodism, theology, ecology

Introduction

There are very few writings about the primacy of relationality and about how John Wesley used such a framework to inform his theology and praxis, not to mention ecological theology. Even *The Cambridge Companion to John Wesley*, with its core goal of "surveying major dimensions of Wesley's activity and writings," does not highlight it.[1] The people called Methodists in the Pacific[2] today struggle to answer the following

1 Randy L. Maddox and Jason E. Vickers, eds., *The Cambridge Companion to John Wesley* (Cambridge: Cambridge University Press, 2010).

2 I have used the term *Pacific* in this chapter for specific reasons. It is a fact that we cannot escape from the term, as it is widely used in many political,

This chapter is a refreshed version of a paper presented at the Oxford Institute of Methodist Theological Studies, Pembroke College, Oxford, 2018.

question: How will Wesley's theology respond to a colonial takeover of our lands, oceans, and peoples? Unlimited material growth is now the true obsession of postmodernity, infiltrating all levels of life in the Pacific at the expense of God's creation. Can Pacific Methodists contribute to an alternative story that restores the harmony of the multiplicity of relationships? Can they create an ecological revolution?

This chapter attempts to reconstruct an eco-relational theology to argue that the concept of relationality is not only at the heart of the Triune God but also at the heart of Wesleyan theology and revival. The aim is to ground theologically a Methodist ecological revolution within the spaces of conflict and climate change hotspots in the Pacific.[3] In this way we can help equip Methodists to contribute, constructively, from a Wesleyan perspective, by finding sustainable alternatives that will save the region in the midst of its colonial

---

economic, social, religious, legal, and educational settings. Moreover, in the everyday life of the people, the word *Pacific* (Pasefika, Pasifika, etc.) is used. However, one needs to decolonize the term to incorporate the holistic ideas of the Oceania and Wansolwara (one ocean). First, the Pacific is "not small and isolated" as assumed by colonizers. The vast *moana*, according to Epeli Hauofa, reveals an interconnected yet diverse race. Second, it does not only refer to the south as in the designation "South Pacific." This is a colonial division that left the south to Northwest Europe and the north to the United States and Northeast Asia. Third, it is not an appendage to Asia as in the "Asia-Pacific" political and economic construct. Designating it as such promotes a land-locked perspective, therefore making the liquid Pacific invisible under Asia, leading to the concealing of the painful stories of the islanders who have suffered under colonial rule. Fourth, it is not romantic as promoted in the tourism sectors. This commercial representation depicts the Pacific as a region without issues that therefore needs to be conquered and developed. Fifth is that the Pacific is not exclusive of the diaspora. For further understanding, see Upolu Lumā Vaai and Aisake Casimira, *Relational Hermeneutics: Decolonising the Mindset and the Pacific Itulagi* (Suva: University of the South Pacific and the Pacific Theological College, 2017), 7–9.

3 Volker Boege, *Climate Change and Conflict in Oceania: Challenges, Responses, and Suggestions for a Policy-Relevant Research Agenda*, Policy Brief no. 17 (Tokyo: Toda Peace Institute, 2018), 1.

takeover. For such a task, this chapter argues that it is critical to rediscover the primacy of relationality that is fundamental to Wesley's theology—informing his ground-up paradigm of life—as well as to the Pacific indigenous worldviews.

Contextual Considerations: Disembodiment and Pacific Methodism

For those in vulnerable and defenseless places such as the small Pacific island communities, there is a desperate need for theologies that reconsider the importance of their life-affirming values of respecting cosmic relationships and interconnectedness. This comes as a response to an urgent call by islanders to find an alternative development story. With regard to one of my brothers from Tuvalu, an island in the Pacific whose highest point is only three meters above sea level, this response is urgent, as "others are enjoying life from our death"[4]—the kind of slow death made possible by unlimited production without ethical limits and reinforced by a human-centric neoliberal capitalist agenda that now infiltrates every aspect of life. Like water flowing into everything, filling every crack and gap of life, the ingrained neoliberal paradigm of growth is offering more ecological death than sustainability, and Methodists are either normalizing such a narrative, allowing it to shape the Pacific political, economic, social, and religious landscapes, or neglecting to treat it as a part of their theological agenda. Making things difficult is that the focus on Wesley's theology that would inform critically ecological discourse, especially climate change, is still given very minimal attention in the regional and the global arena. The result is the inability of many Methodists to deal with a destructive economic development narrative that allows for ecological violence.

---

4 Falemanuka Maitoga, "Climate Change in Tuvalu," presentation to Theology of Disasters class, Pacific Theological College, Suva, Fiji, 2017.

"Christian faith is always *embodied* faith," argues Andrew Walls, if Christianity is to make a definitive difference in the Pacific.[5] The very struggle for Pacific Methodism to critique the mainstream development narrative is due to disembodiment.[6] When a faith is not fully embodied in the contextual *itulagi*[7] of the believer, the Pacific cultures and contexts that inform their thinking and life, then faith becomes more and more a heavenly business. The risks are not only the abstract speculation and misunderstanding of such faith, but also an uncritical submission to a church tradition that has limited or no resources for dealing with the real, painful stories of communities pushed to the margins by a dominant economic system. This meaning-making strategy must also go beyond the notion of relevancy in which inculturation and contextual theologies have been mired. The faith that we seek to understand more deeply must also be able to provide a rethinking and revolutionary environment that promotes the courage to speak and act against the destructive and painful colonial hegemonies, both past and present, of these marginal communities—that is, an anti-imperial

5 Andrew Walls, "Theology and Broader Reflections, Methodists, Missions and Pacific Christianity: A New Chapter in Christian History," in *Weaving the Unfinished Mats: Wesley's Legacy—Conflict, Confusion and Challenge in the South Pacific*, edited by Peter Lineham (Auckland: Proceedings of the Wesley Historical Society Conference, 2007), 14.

6 Upolu Lumā Vaai, "Itiiti a lega mea—Less yet More! A Pacific Relational Development Paradigm of Life," in Vaai and Casimira, *Relational Hermeneutics*, 215–31.

7 *Itulagi* is a Samoan word that literally means "side of the heavens" or "side of the horizon." Any perspective is defined by one's side or contextual lifeworld. A person has many *itu* or sides that make up one's side of the heavens. These *itu* constitute the "baggage" that conditions one's thinking, including culture, family, religion, people, land, ancestors, ocean, language, spirits, and even the *tuālagi* (universe). Recognizing these diverse realities that make up our side of the heavens suggests that our consciousness always operates in a world of meanings that is culturally and historically conditioned. These *itu* make up the context out of which we construct knowledge, experience life, and understand the world around them without fear of betrayal. This is why every perspective is limited, because it is always from one's "side of the heavens."

environment where we, in the light of the subversive God of faith, are able to "hear their cry" in the midst of a loud, materialistic extractive culture and "know their suffering" in the midst of an institutionalized human-centric system of power (Exod. 3:7).

Disembodiment is one of the greatest challenges that the Pacific people face today. This is especially true because we find ourselves in a region that has for many years developed a dependent mentality not only on imported goods but also on imported frameworks and models shaped by Eurocentric constitutional democracies.[8] Disembodiment is a colonial construct. Colonization is rooted in the word *colon,* which in both Latin and Greek means a "digestive system." Colonialism is when the powerful one, whether a person, community, or organization, desires to create and protect a digestive system that consumes more power, more money, more wealth, and more resources at the expense of the many, including God's creation.[9] Disembodiment is the manifestation of the colonial "one truth" ideology, with an emphasis on only one digestive center of thinking, one digestive way of doing things, and one digestive interpretation of God.[10]

When Christianity was struggling to make sense of the divine incarnation of Jesus Christ within the Greco-Roman Empire dominated by the one truth ideology, the result was that Christian theology and its philosophical mechanistic and monarchical orientation became the comfortable home for such ideology, with the church as its breeding ground.[11] Consequently, in such theology God has to be understood outside of the embodied life of the grassroots communities. For

---

8 Graham Hassall, "Democracy in the Pacific: Tensions between Systems and Lifeworld," in *A Region in Transition: Politics and Power in Pacific Island Countries*, ed. A. Holtz, M. Kawasch, and O. Hasenkamp (Saarbrücken: Saarland University Press, 2016), 313.

9 Upolu Lumā Vaai, introduction to Vaai and Casimira, *Relational Hermeneutics,* 1–14.

10 See Upolu Lumā Vaai, "A Theology of Talalasi: Challenging the 'One Truth Ideology' of the Empire," *Pacific Journal of Theology* 55 (2016): 50–62.

11 Laurel Schneider, *Beyond Monotheism: A Theology of Multiplicity* (London: Routledge, 2008), 17.

centuries in theological institutions in the Pacific, for example, theological education promoted the idea that only when a local theology or interpretation is validated by a Eurocentric set of standards and methods can it become universally accepted. Local theologies, fully shaped by the local context and epistemologies, could not be seen as sufficient unless they satisfy the requirements of these standards controlled by an invisible center of knowledge somewhere outside of the Pacific.

The basic example of this is that theological education in the Pacific for centuries has been pushing students to think and theologize in the light of systems and categories that belong to the Western philosophical tradition and epistemologies and not in terms of multiple interconnected relationships fundamental to Pacific epistemologies. When I attended a local Methodist theological institution, oral histories and stories were dismissed, as they did not fit into this Western production of knowledge that controls the school's curriculum. This is because the curriculum promoted literary form as the only legitimate mode of documenting and passing down theological knowledge. In my twenty plus years of experience in theological education as a Pacific Methodist, I have seen and experienced in many places I work the inherent racism couched in one-dimensional theological frameworks and curricula.

Eurocentric knowledge fears indigenous oral knowledge because of its openness to complexity and multidimensionality. Most often Pacific epistemologies are attuned to complex structures of knowledge and relationships rather than to just one simple defined system of knowledge. These complex structures are transmitted through stories, arts, rituals, idioms, and metaphors, to name a few. Oral traditions bring alive the complex histories and memories that are not present in archives, books, and other forms of literary traditions. They act as conduits of knowledge that inform the spirituality of the people in relation to their lands and oceans. In this sense, the literary form is only one dimension of this complex knowledge structure. So for Methodism to teach and uphold that there is only a single mode of knowledge not only gives warrant to a theological and educational colonial takeover but also suppresses the free flow of grace that opens up the multiple dimensions of God's presence in all cultures and peoples.

Two things happen as a result of colonial disembodiment. First, it limits the flow of God's free grace that embraces the indigenous and local. Free grace was the subversive Wesleyan take on the kind of disembodied and institutionalized religion that was in vogue during his time, wherein God was boxed according to standards and criteria set by a one-dimensional Christian orthodoxy. The marginal communities with which John Wesley was concerned were taught that accessibility to this God is something that the institutional church alone can offer. Second, it set the stage for the organized eroding of the cosmological and eco-relational worldview of Pacific communities in the name of a universal God and the centrality of the human being.

Disembodiment is particularly obvious when it comes to Methodism's long focus on the saving of souls. Many Methodists have translated this missional focus to be human-centric. The Pacific today is overwhelmed with many issues that find their roots in a human centric economic development paradigm that does not recognize any ecological soul. In the Pacific worldview, by contrast, everything is alive within a living eco-relational household and therefore has a soul. Ecology does not refer only to the nonhuman world as promoted in the West following Ernst Haeckel, who also coined the word *ecology*. This has become a fashionable term used by environmentalists to mean that the earth has its own dynamic ecological system that is beyond human imagination. While this is true, it also set the stage for a nonrelational, compartmentalized narrative where ecology refers only to the natural environment. The neoliberal capitalist philosophy of growth thrives within this one-dimensional narrative, because one of its goals is to split the human from the earth for extraction purposes. For this reason, extraction goes in two different directions. On the one hand, the earth is viewed as an externality, subject to the uncontrollable extractive capitalist culture, while on the other hand, the Haeckel-influenced ecologists, in protesting against destroying the earth, pursue a strategy of continuing to split the human and the earth, resulting in their inability to critically address the core of such destruction, which is human-centric economy.

This human-centric philosophy of growth promotes the "more is better" development paradigm, where the concepts of moreness, increase, and growth are placed against concepts such as lessness, decrease, and loss. The more we extract and produce, the better the economy. To have less is often viewed as an economic loss. While the language of minus and having less is often associated with Christian sharing and mutual caring in many indigenous communities, people today connect not because of sharing but rather because of competition for growth over limited resources that the already vulnerable communities have. It is unfortunate that governments in the region have normalized the idea of borrowing capitalist economic models, such as the gross domestic product (GDP), rooted in the "more is better" paradigm, to measure well-being. The healthier the GDP, the better the people, it seems.[12] Unfortunately, this is not the case. The economies of the countries in the Global South are suffering, while many of their resources are being moved to improve the lifestyles of the powerful, including many in the Global North. These imported economic models promote the fracturing of interconnectedness of the whole and promote an endless extractive obsession at the expense of all other members of the eco-relational household. Hence it has fostered communities that worship and serve Caesar, the life-taking god of the market empire.[13]

With the notion of life-taking directly or indirectly shaping every part of our development consciousness, we who follow this market god no longer feel grief, love, or suffering. Because the dominant economic system does not have a soul, therefore it goes against anything that emphasizes emotions and deep spiritual connections. This is why many

---

12 For full discussion of how the Pacific is affected by the neoliberal philosophy of growth, see, for example, Upolu Lumā Vaai, *We Are Therefore We Live: Eco-relational Spirituality and Changing the Climate Change Story*, Policy Brief no. 56 (Tokyo: Toda Peace Institute, 2019).

13 Joerg Rieger, *Jesus vs Caesar: For People Tired of Serving the Wrong God* (Nashville: Abingdon, 2018).

growth-instilled people no longer mourn the severe distortions caused by the commodification of God-given gifts such as land, ocean, rivers, animals, and trees. They no longer feel that life-taking and murdering other members of our eco-relational household is a sin, because our thinking is no longer guided by life-affirming values but rather by policies and legal frameworks that serve the market ideology. Pope Francis lamented the loss of this deep, emotional spiritual connection that "we have forgotten that we ourselves are dust of the earth (cf. Gen 2:7); our very bodies are made up of her elements, we breathe her air and we receive life and refreshment from her waters."[14] When we lose remembrance, especially the memory of deep connection, we lose what it means to live within our means. As a result, we carry every day the sin of living beyond our means. It is a sin because we no longer recognize others in our lives by taking what belongs to them to consolidate our own. This is a serious and organized crime, orchestrated against poor and marginal communities, and we often warrant it with policy and regulatory justification, allowing it to develop a system and context to cultivate. Hence hidden in most economic systems is the systemic sin against marginal communities that goes unnoticed every day.

The desire for wealth without ethical limits has inevitably contributed to a vulnerable Pacific that is overwhelmed by environmental issues, climate injustice, policies that marginalize indigenous people from their lands and resources, militarization and political colonization, the rapid pace of poverty and unemployment, the culture of resource extraction as in the recent threat of deep-sea mining, and the undeniable geopolitical competition and presence in the region of rich and powerful countries as well as transnational fishing and mining corporations that heavily invest in countries addicted to debt yet without the means to pay back these debts. The challenge is: How can Wesley's theology inform an alternative paradigm that is able to modify human development within the contours of eco-relationality?

---

14 Pope Francis, *Encyclical Letter, Laudato Si of the Holy Father Francis on Care for Our Common Home* (Strathfield, NSW: St Paul's, 2015), 10.

It is a risky business to link current thinking with Wesley's theology, especially since he did not appeal to eco-relationality as part of his theological vocabulary. Some would argue that we should be careful about imposing our contemporary thinking on Wesley, because the nonhuman world was not high on his theological agenda.[15] However what is even riskier is if this tendency would prevent Methodists from pursuing constant theological renewal. The challenge for Methodism today is the taking of risks, if Methodism is to be relevant and to remain within the category of the three Rs: revival, reform, and revolution. Such risks are not about the imposing of the new on the old, but rather about refreshing the old with the new.

Two things are worth considering if we want an embodied Methodism that includes an eco-relationality. First, although relationality was not part of Wesley's language, at the heart of his theology was his faith in the relationality of God as expressed in God's free grace for all. His emphasis on social religion and social holiness, which appears across all of his theological thinking, testifies to this central point. To Wesley "the gospel of Christ knows of no religion, but social; no holiness but social holiness."[16] While I personally do not like the word *social,* as it could invite a dichotomy between the social and the private, something that does not really appear in the Pacific relational worldview, Wesley's focus was that "social religion is a matter of being in *relationship* with God and with others, and it is a public matter."[17]

The primacy of relationality is the underlying principle of a religion that knows no boundaries—social religion. Influences from Catholic, Reformed, Anglican, Eastern Orthodox, Pietist, and Arminian

15 Theodore Runyon, *The New Creation: John Wesley's Theology Today* (Nashville: Abingdon, 1998), 200.

16 John and Charles Wesley, "List of Poetical Works," cited by Rieger, *No Religion but Social Religion: Liberating Wesleyan Theology* (Nashville: General Board of Higher Education and Ministry, 2018), vii.

17 Rieger, *No Religion but Social Religion,* viii. Emphasis added.

traditions all shaped Wesley to speak of the relational terms of salvation.[18] That variety of salvation is about having right relationship with God and with one's neighbor. And for Wesley, because of God's grace, God is the author and initiator of such relationships.

Second, if Methodism is to answer to the cry of Pacific marginal communities that *others are enjoying life from our death,* the way to make sure Wesley's theology provides a constructive response is to reframe it in a contextual hermeneutical perspective. Relational hermeneutics allows the present receiver, such as Pacific marginal communities, to reconstruct and creatively reproduce Wesley's theology to address their plight, while being critical of their own contexts so that what is received is not so much a theological idea from the past but rather the living God of faith.

The Ecological Misconception

Fighting for eco-justice is a challenge, especially because when many of us talk about relationship or relationality, our mind-sets immediately go straight to either the God-human relationship or to interhuman relationships. The multiple nonhuman relationships are often relegated as secondary to the God-human relationship. Hence most of the literature and scholarship about relationality produced in and from the West mainly concern the human-centric, which is why sometimes the eco-relational worldview is either misunderstood by the romantics or condemned by Western academics.

For example, sometimes eco-relationality, with its principles such as the sacredness and connectedness of all things, is misjudged and selectively labeled by some as belonging to "dark green religion" or to environmentalism that worships the environment at the exclusion of all other aspects of life, including God.[19] While I agree that the notion of inter-

18 For a further understanding of how these traditions shaped Wesley's theological career, see Jason E. Vickers, "Wesley's Theological Emphases," in Maddox and Vickers, *Cambridge Companion to John Wesley*, 190–206.

19 Bron Taylor, *Dark Green Religion: Nature Spirituality and the Planetary Future* (Berkeley: University of California Press, 2010), ix–x.

connectedness can sometimes be twisted to serve communality at the expense of individuality or bent for political and economic reasons, as discussed above, where people are connected only through competition for a few resources, eco-relationality should not be limited to worship, as it is more about "deep connection" and continuity. It is about deep mutual connection with the vulnerable peoples and places in small island marginal communities such as the Pacific who first feel the impact of climate change and bear the heavy brunt of environmental violence.

While some recently produced relational theologies offer some glimpse of hope, again they are enslaved by the human-centric worldview. This is especially seen when the relationality of God is framed in what is often called in the West a personalistic view of God over and against an absolutistic view. Many Methodists would favor the former over the latter. However, while this view brings God closer to us to highlight love as central to a personal God, it still runs the risk of boxing God within a dominant human-centric cultural construct where the nonhuman world is viewed as secondary to the primacy of the God-human relationship.[20] Emphasizing God's deep relationship to the nonhuman world can also help us address other theological problems, like humanizing God to the extent of making God in our human image and then worshiping that very image, which Justo L. González warned about thirty years ago.[21] This definitely neglects the encompassing role of the Holy Spirit that is foundational to Wesleyan spirituality, the very force that allows the Triune God to relate to and intimately connect with all of creation.

---

20 See, for example, Barry L. Callen, "John Wesley and Relational Theology," in *Relational Theology: A Contemporary Introduction*, ed. Brint Montgomery, Thomas J. Oord, and Karen Strand Winslow (Eugene, OR: Wipf and Stock, 2012), 7–10. In this book, the God-human relationship is highlighted with minimal treatment given to the natural environment, except for the last two chapters, which is often the case with many theology projects.

21 Justo L. González, *Mãnana: Christian Theology from a Hispanic Perspective* (Nashville: Abingdon, 1990), 90.

It is also not enough to say, as Matthew Seaman claims, that "Wesley's main focus was certainly on equality among humans, however, this can be extended to all creatures and potentially all of earth."[22] This is still a problematic take on Wesley, where the nonhuman world is treated as an appendage or an extension to a human-centric theology. In the eco-relational worldview, there is no such thing as extensions. We are all equally part of the eco-relational household where fullness of life for all is at the heart of existence.

The basic question is: How can Wesley's God become a God of all rather than just of humans? *All* is Wesley's magic word.[23] How can we redefine this encompassing *all-ness* to make sure we do not confine Wesley's theology to the human-centric? Especially to the church? We need to firmly establish a theological response to environmental violence and destruction grounded in Wesley's wealth of theological wisdom, or else Methodists will continue to be unresponsive when demands arise for sustainable solutions to environmental issues that affect their societies.

As discussed above, with the Eurocentric narrative, where ecology refers only to the natural environment, God and the human being exist outside of ecology. Two reasons for such invention can be highlighted here. On the one hand, to protect God's identity, God has to be theologically engineered in a way that any divine deep involvement as part of the ecological structure has to be carefully prevented from impacting God's divinity and power. In Wesley's time, divine "deep involvement" was deeply problematic due to a mechanistic philosophy of God, where the relational life-giving God of the Bible gradually lost uniqueness in favor of a Supreme Being who rules and judges the world from above.[24] Beginning in the Enlightenment, God was often defined and

22 Mathew Seaman, "Dark Green Religion and the Wesleyan Tradition: Harmony and Dissonance," *Wesleyan Theological Journal* 48 (2013): 142.

23 John Wesley, "Free Grace," in *The Works of John Wesley*, vol. 3, *Sermons III, 71–114*, ed. Albert C. Outler (Nashville: Abingdon, 1986), 542–63.

24 Marc Otto and Michael Lodahl, "'We Cannot Know Much, but We May Love Much': Mystery and Humility in John Wesley's Narrative Ecology," *Wesleyan Theological Journal* 44 (2009): 118–40.

understood in terms of power and influence. A God that has no power and influence is a God that cannot be trusted. As a result, Christianity during Wesley's time became victim to what Wes Howard-Brook calls the "religion of the empire."[25] To be a religion of the empire means to deny the contextual embodiment of God in different contexts and diverse cultures. Against this anti-incarnational and non-relational idea of God, Wesley instead brought back into the church and society a more freely relational, interactive God, who is not confined to a center of power or thinking. For Wesley the grace of God is key to understanding divine deep involvement, and the Spirit makes that possible from beginning to end.

On the other hand, when human beings are the representatives of this mechanistic God, their role has to be theologically engineered as the "overseers" of the nonhuman world, something that was made popular since the scientific advancements of the Enlightenment. By giving that privilege to themselves, not only did the human beings claim special treatment apart from the nonhuman world, but because of this framing, the *oikos* triplets of economy, ecology, and *oikoumene* were slowly split apart. Like the stolen generation of Australia, ecology was stolen by the scientific empire, turned into a mere object that can be extracted, and stripped in order to be objectively studied and researched. Economy was stolen by the capitalist empire, stripped of its original role of managing a home, and turned into a money-making machine that serves the interest of a few. Economy is today becoming an amoral machine that acts separately from ecology. The more it does, the more immoral it becomes. And *oikoumene* was stolen by the Christian empire and turned into a human-centric system that serves the interest of Christians who see themselves as a fellowship and unity under Christ that has nothing to do with ecology. Hence economy and ecology were hardly featured as part of ecumenical discussions nor seen to be central to ecumenical theology.

---

25 Wes Howard-Brook, *Empire Baptized: How the Church Embraced What Jesus Rejected (Second–Fifth Centuries)* (Maryknoll, NY: Orbis, 2016).

With the uncontrollable extraction by capitalist humans of natural resources, another theology was proposed by the church, the theology of stewardship, which suggests that humans should act as caretakers of ecology. What is now normalized in our mind-sets is that stewardship is all about human acts of fixing and/or saving the natural environment. This can be done by exercising self-limitation, for instance.[26] The problem with this view is that while we worry about saving the natural environment, we are never connected to it. The fundamental question is: Can we honestly take care of something that we are never connected to?

Eco-relational Theology and Wesley

For an embodied Methodism, it is important to place Wesleyan theology within the contours of relational hermeneutics that informs the thinking of the Pacific communities. Relational hermeneutics acknowledges the fact that relationality is the overarching core value that encompasses all of life. However, it is not limited to the Pacific, for an encompassing and holistic relationality embraces all relationships, including the nonhuman world. It is the interpretive key to life and well-being for many indigenous first peoples around the world. With such a complex and diverse region as the Pacific, relationality is translated and contextualized to fit all the contexts and lifeworlds of the region. Hence relationality has different faces depending on its cultural and contextual location. Pacific communities believe that relationality is not one-dimensional or human-centric. It is a complex, multidimensional, and cosmological whole. It sees the world as a complex cosmic community that includes God, human beings, others, and the environment that are the elusive constellations of embodied life.[27]

---

26 Sharon R. Harvey, "God's Relation to Nature," in Montgomery, Oord, and Winslow, *Relational Theology*, 113–115.

27 For more on Pacific relationality, see Upolu Lumā Vaai and Unaisi Nabobo-Baba, eds., *The Relational Self: Decolonising Personhood in the Pacific* (Suva: University of the South Pacific and the Pacific Theological College, 2017).

It is also important to acknowledge that Pacific cultures, like any other, are prone to corruption and colonial distortion. One must not overlook the fact that any culture can be maneuvered to prop up the power structures of either a controlling majority or an influential minority. The role of relational hermeneutics is to encourage a critical, hermeneutical, and unified process of *liuliu* (deconstruction), *liliu* (reconstruction), and *toe liuliu* (return to restart the process).[28] These three hermeneutical phases, borrowed from my own tradition, the Samoan wisdom process, are important for analyzing critically our constantly changing cultures. This would give us confidence to say that what comes out of the local, shaped by the local communities' worldview, might not be perfect, but it is perhaps the most sustainable compared to what is borrowed. It is sustainable because it is borne from the ground-up worldviews of the marginal communities. However, a critical hermeneutical process, where the role of the Spirit is central, must be put in place to critically examine this local turn.

The reason environmental destruction is not easily accepted by most indigenous communities, like those in the Pacific, is because in their eco-relational worldview, the natural environment is perceived as their *tino* (body). For Pacific indigenous people, the people and the earth can only exist in relation to the other. The earth is more than just a piece of dirt. It is family. It is *in* us. The cosmic community is in us, and we are in the cosmic community.[29] For example, in Samoa, the word for soil (*eleele*) is the same as the word for blood. The word for the earth (*palapala*) is another word for blood. *Ua tafe le palapala* (blood is spilled) means that the earth loses life whenever there is bloodshed. The word for placenta (*fanua*) is the same as the word for land. The word for the rocks/stones (*fatu*) is the same word as for the human heart. The word for the skies (*lagi*) is also used for a human head. The word for

---

28 Vaai and Casimira, *Relational Hermeneutics*, 23–24.

29 Upolu Lumā Vaai, "Vaatapalagi: De-heavening Trinitarian Theology in the Islands," in *Colonial Contexts and Postcolonial Theologies: Storyweaving in the Asia-Pacific*, edited by Mark Brett and Jione Havea (New York: Palgrave Macmillan, 2014), 41–53.

roots of a tree (*a'a*) is the same word for human genealogy. The word for human skull (*atigisami*) is the same word as for a seashell, connoting that wisdom is always connected to the ocean currents, flows, and turbulences. The word for tongue (*laulaufaiva*) connotes distribution of resources rather than digestion. When a mother tree or a hub tree is cut, the word used is *oia*, meaning "the whole forest cries in pain." This is why any cutting of hub trees should be accompanied by rituals to ask for pardon and to restore balance, as the whole forest will be affected from cutting just one tree. When the newborn's umbilical cord (*pute*) is severed, a ritual is performed to bury this in the ground to reconnect the newborn to the land of ancestors. This deep connection is supposed to be carried and honored by human beings throughout their lives. In eco-relational worldviews, balance and harmony are not romantic notions as profiled in the Global North but rather intergenerational ecological principles designed to protect the multiple relationships within the eco-relational household.

This means that a human being is ecological through and through. There is no disconnection of earth and people. Ecology touches on every aspect of life, from the human being to economy, to religion, to language, even to God. When we miss this eco-relationality of the whole, we miss the point that everything is interconnected and woven together like a mat. I am a walking land! A moving earth! As Fijians say, *tamata ni vanua, vanua ni tamata* (the land is the people and the people are the land). This saying outlines the deep relationship of the people and the natural environment. Epeli Hau'ofa from Tonga once coined the well-known phrase "We are the Ocean, the Ocean is Us."[30] Following Hau'ofa, Teresia Teaiwa said that "we sweat and cry salt so we know that the ocean is really in our blood."[31] Pope Francis calls this kind of deep connection "integral ecology," which allows us

30 Epeli Hau'ofa, "Our Sea of Islands," in *A New Oceania: Rediscovering Our Sea of Islands,* ed. Eric Waddell, Vijay Naidu, and Epeli Hau'ofa (Suva: University of the South Pacific, 1993), 2–16.

31 Teresia Teaiwa, quoted in Epeli Hau'ofa, *We Are the Ocean: Selected Works* (Honolulu: University of Hawaii, 2008), 41.

to see the earth as family: "Our common home is like a sister with whom we share our life and a beautiful mother who opens her arms to embrace us."[32] For Pacific communities, anything that is body-related, that they belong to, that is part of them, they will protect and care for. This also goes with Christianity, including Methodism. As a matter of fact, this idea of integral ecology existed in the Pacific, and in many indigenous communities, long before Pope Francis made reference to it.

To reconstruct a theology of stewardship in light of these traditions means that saving the natural environment through self-limitation and all other stewardship acts cannot work unless we feel we are intimately part of what we are trying to save. Our mind-sets need to shift from the stewardship idea of caring for the earth that has dominated Eurocentric theology to living with the earth. In the Pacific eco-relational perspective, relating precedes the caring. Before we carry the earth in our hands, we have to carry it in our hearts. Honest and empathetic stewarding means that once we (re)discover that intimate emotional and spiritual connection through *living with* the earth, the *caring for* should follow. Stewardship is about deep connection that is always spiritual in nature.[33] To be there and to care for the earth should start with the resolve to be with. We can only honestly love and care for the earth if we are deeply connected to it.

Eco-relationality maintains that while one is *en-othered* (moving toward affirming communality), one still enjoys real freedom to be oneself. And while the community is *en-selfed* (moving toward affirming individuality in the community), it still enjoys real freedom as a community. This *en-otherness* of the one for the sake of the many and the *en-selfness* of the many for the sake of the one is a Trinitarian structure of life that is part of cultures that emphasize eco-relationality. Hence in these cultures, the Trinity is not a mere doctrine. It is a way of being and of life already present in our everyday *en-selfness* of the many

32 Pope Francis, *Laudato Si,* 1, 16.

33 For Wesley's notion of stewardship, see his sermon 51, "The Good Steward," in *Works of John Wesley,* 2:282–98.

and *en-otherness* of the individual, grounded in the love relationship of God through Christ in the Spirit. In the eco-relational worldview, God does not divide the sacred and secular, spirit and flesh, communality and individuality, or church and world as we usually do. All are woven together into an inextricable whole. Eco-relationality means that the Trinitarian relationship is wholly part of our everyday eco-relationships. There is no such thing as intra-Trinitarian relationship "in God" (immanent Trinity) as opposed to social Trinitarian relationship "God present to the outside" (economic Trinity). There is only a relational God of love who is *en-selfed* yet freely communal and *en-othered* yet freely distinct. This outpouring of love to both the individual and the community would mean for Wesley that his understanding of revival is not so much about a revival of the church but rather the revival of relationality found in the flow of grace from the self to the community and from the community to the self.

This relational perspective provides the lens, at least for Pacific Methodists, to understand why Wesley shifted from a theology that focuses on the existence of God, confined by the power dynamics of the empire, to a theology that embraces an existence of multiple relationships in God. From a relational perspective, all of us are meant to exist in harmonious relationships in a living eco-relational household, where life and resources are meant to be shared and flow from one to the other in an *en-selfed* and *en-othered* way. In such a household, while humans have different designs from that of the trees, land, and ocean, we are all diversely connected through an ecological reference.

Therefore nothing exists outside of such reference. Human beings are believed to be ecologically formed. As a Pacific Methodist, I carry within me the terrestrial, oceanic, and ancestral dynamics that form who I am. The environment is meant to be ecologically structured. Communities and societies should be ecologically ordered. Our languages are meant to be ecologically nuanced. Even God ecologically modifies God's self through the work of the Spirit in order to be part of the eco-relational household. This ecological reference informs us that eco-relationality is like a strand that connects all of us human beings as well as our activities to the soil, ocean, water, trees, sky, and God. We are undivided in separate distinct bodies. Because of this reality, when one is affected, all are affected. When one suffers, all suffer (1 Cor. 12:26). This is the Trinitarian structure of life, according to Gregory of Nazianzus, a Cappadocian father who certainly influenced Wesley. We cannot understand the Trinity unless we understand mutuality. When we speak of one, we speak of the whole, because one is mutually included in the whole.[34]

The primacy of relationality found its way into Wesley's thinking in that he was more interested in how God relates than how God exists. One could argue that this theological emphasis of Wesley was drawn from the Eastern Orthodox tradition. Since Albert Outler in the mid-1960s suggested a connection between Wesley's theology and the Cappadocian fathers, many debates have surfaced that engage such a claim.[35] Whatever the outcome, it is hard to deny the influence of the Eastern patristic fathers on Wesley's relational terms of salvation. This is obvious in how Wesley approached the doctrine of the Trinity, despite the fact that he was careful of using the word *Trinity*, as it is not found in the Bible.[36] In his sermon "On the Trinity," Wesley argues that God's revelation is "at the very heart of Christianity" and that "the knowledge of the Three-One God," the Father, the Son, and the Spirit, "is interwoven with all true Christian faith."[37] This means that for Wesley, knowledge of God does not start with what was challenged by systematic theologian Catherine Mowry LaCugna, namely a rational piercing into the "inner life of

---

34 Gregory of Nazianzus, *Orations* 40.41, in *A Select Library of Nicene and Post-Nicene Fathers*, second series, vol. 7, ed. Phillip Scharff and Henry Wace (Grand Rapids, MI: Eerdmans, 1978), 375.

35 Albert C. Outler, ed., *John Wesley* (New York: Oxford University Press, 1964), 9–10. See especially footnote on page 9. For the debates, see, for example, Ted A. Campbell, "Wesley's Use of the Church Fathers," *Asbury Theological Journal* 50 (1995): 57–70.

36 John Wesley, sermon 54, "On the Trinity," in *Works of John Wesley*, 2:378.

37 Ibid., 2:384–85.

God," about which we know nothing. Rather it is woven together with how God relates to us through Christ in the Spirit in the economy of salvation.[38]

We find in this divine relationality the fact that God has to move out of God's self through Christ, not so much to relate, as God is already relational, but rather to affirm to us the way God works. That is, God's moving toward us (*en-otherness*) does not in any way compromise God's divine identity (*en-selfness*). Rather it is the very thing that affirms it. This divine paradox is key to understanding the deep involvement of God. It is also key to understanding how we, made in the light of the relationality of God, can only be ourselves when we include those who are not us. In other words, it is relationality that may lead us to discover more about the mystery of the divine, despite that we do so brokenly, as Wesley would have put it. And in this discovery, we may find that a God-driven relationship is critical to a grace-driven salvation.

This is why Wesley, in my view, does not draw up a definite number of fundamental systematic doctrines, as for him, relationship is fundamental. He believes that everything, including religion, should come from a relationship that begins with God and is communicated by the Spirit to all. In his sermon "The Way to the Kingdom," he puts it this way: "For neither does religion consist in orthodoxy or right opinions," continuing that a person "may think justly concerning the incarnation of our Lord, concerning the ever blessed Trinity, and every other doctrine contained in the creeds . . . and yet 'tis possible he may have no religion at all."[39] Wesley is not discarding orthodoxy, yet he thinks that without the love of deep involvement, orthodoxy finds no meaning. At the heart of orthodoxy is the primacy of divine involvement. Hence the comprehensibility of orthodoxy is found in its performability.

---

38 Catherine Mowry LaCugna, *God for Us: The Trinity and Christian Life* (New York: HarperCollins, 1991).

39 John Wesley, sermon 7, "The Way to the Kingdom," in *Works of John Wesley*, 1:220.

Perhaps Wesley saw into the future that when orthodoxy is detached from performance, it can easily become a warrant to justify power structures. For example, the doctrine of the Trinity in the Pacific, because of its misconception, was and is still used to justify the colonization of spaces and people in the name of God. When God is understood as omnipotent and omniscient, this is normally translated to mean a deity who exists in deep isolation, who only approves of relations that prop up the power structures of the status quo. When the event of the cross is understood as the passive, silent obedience of Jesus to appease a powerful God of sacrifices, we have a theology that warrants the hierarchical power of God represented by a dominant system that exploits the silent Jesus represented by vulnerable communities and individuals. Thus the greatest sin that we have to deal with is our thirst for power where we go to great lengths to protect systems and structures that secure such power, despite its destructive impact on the many, including the natural environment.

Concluding Remarks

A shift from eco-theology to eco-relational theology is an ecological revolution grounded on the primacy of the relationality of God, something that Wesley always emphasized. For Wesley it is this relational grounding that allowed him to be theologically innovative and practically relational. It allowed him to go beyond the dominant narrative of his time to challenge not only the existing center of power but also the existing theological basis that justified such power, which is God. It also allowed him to believe that God's free grace "is all in all,"[40] which led him to a life of deep connection and deep involvement with society, especially with poor grassroots communities. Wesley frequently uses the phrase "solitary religion" to put the spotlight on what he calls "social religion," which is more about the relationality of grace that is never limited and cannot be confined to institutionalized structures.

40 Wesley, "Free Grace," 3:544.

To Wesley "Christianity is essentially a social religion, and to turn it into a solitary one is to destroy it."[41] What would this mean to a Methodist Church that calls itself the body of Christ within a vulnerable and exposed region such as the Pacific? How would Wesley's sense of allness shape the way we see mission in a broader way that includes the nonhuman world?

The primacy of relationality would also assist in decolonizing of our mind-sets and help us to see that our inability to uphold complexity and the fracturing and destruction of multiple relations, including the natural environment, is against God's will. Sustainability of life is possible not only through the embracing and strengthening of complex multiple relations that include the nonhuman world. It is also about reestablishing and reconnecting with the whole of creation. It will also help Pacific Methodism understand the importance of engaging in social and environmental justice movements and advocacies.

Most important, the Spirit for Wesley enables the relationality of God in our lives. It also makes possible the revolutionary spirit of transformation and newness. With the absence of the Spirit, relationality would be stagnant and could be easily converted to a tool that supports the hierarchy and the abuse of power. It could also be a way to solidify false relationalities such as those that exist within capitalism covered by the myth of individualism and that are already firmly established within our own institutions and ministerial formation. To emphasize eco-relationality is to emphasize the revolutionary role of the Spirit from beginning to end. The Spirit is synonymous both with revolution and newness, making possible the free flow of the grace of God, who continually draws us to celebrate and embrace the diverse rhythms and multidimensional movements of life within the eco-relational family. According to Leonardo Boff, "To think of the Spirit is to think of movement, action, process, appearance, story, and the irruption of something new and surprising. It means

41 John Wesley, sermon 24, "Upon Our Lord's Sermon on the Mount: Discourse the Fourth," in *Works of John Wesley*, 1:533.

thinking about what we are constantly becoming."[42] In this light an ecological revolution through an eco-relational theology is something that will not only shake up our theologies of God and notions of orthodoxy. It will also surely upset the possessive and life-taking mentality we develop in our daily engagement with Caesar, the god of the empire.

42 Leonardo Boff, *Come Holy Spirit: Inner Fire, Giver of Life and Comforter of the Poor* (Maryknoll, NY: Orbis, 2015), viii.

Contributors

Timothy R. Eberhart is associate professor of theology and ecology at Garrett-Evangelical Theological Seminary, where he directs the MA in public ministry degree and oversees a concentration in ecological regeneration. His publications include *Rooted and Grounded in Love: Holy Communion for the Whole Creation* (2017) and *The Economy of Salvation: Essays in Honor of M. Douglas Meeks* (2015). He is an ordained elder in the United Methodist Church, a trained permaculturalist, UMC Earthkeeper, North American secretary for the Oxford Institute of Methodist Theological Studies, and cochair of the Institute for Christian Socialism.

Kisitu Gyaviira holds a PhD in systematic theology from the University of KwaZulu-Natal. He is a postdoctoral fellow at the same university. He has authored various research articles focusing on gender and sexuality, religion and governance. His most recent book chapter is "When Sacrament [ology] and Ubuntu Kiss: Probing the Relationship between Sacraments and the African Concept of Ubuntu" in *Liturgy and Identity*, edited by Lilian C Siwila & Roderick Hewitt (Pietermaritzburg: Cluster Publications, 2018) 121–34. He is also working for the Centre for Constructive Theology as a researcher and project coordinator. He teaches courses in practical theology and systematic theology at the University of KwaZulu-Natal.

R. Simangaliso Kumalo is associate professor of public theology and history at the School of Religion, Philosophy and Classics, University of KwaZulu-Natal Pietermaritzburg. He is also the current head of the Department of Theology and Ethics at the university. He is also former president of Seth Mokitimi Methodist Seminary. He is an ordained elder in the Methodist Church of South Africa. Among his books are *Methodists with a White History and a Black Future: The Story of the People called Methodists in KwaZulu-Natal* (2009) and *Pastor and Politician: Essays on the Life, Work and Legacy of JL Dube, the First President of the African National Congress* (2012). His most recent book is *African Legends of Methodism: Life Stories of Some Leaders Formed by the Methodist Church in Southern Africa* (2020).

Filipe Maia is assistant professor of theology at Boston University School of Theology. He is a coconvener of the webinar series "Decolonizing the Wesleyan Traditions" and author of the forthcoming book chapters: "Alter-carnation: Notes on Cannibalism and Coloniality in the Brazilian Context," in *In the Image of Man: Race, Coloniality, and Philosophy of Religion,* ed. An Yountae and Eleanor Craig, and "Betrayed by Accent: Theological Notes on a Racist Worldsound," in *Toward Sustainable Societies: Interreligious, Interdisciplinary Responses,* ed. Rita Sherma and Purushottama Bilimoria.

Keegan Osinski is the librarian for theology and ethics at Vanderbilt Divinity Library. She has a BA in philosophy and theology from Point Loma Nazarene University, an MLIS from the University of Washington, and an MTS from Vanderbilt Divinity School. She is a member of the Church of the Nazarene.

Pablo Guillermo Oviedo is professor of theology, church history, and mission at the University of the Latin American Educational Center (UCEL), Rosario, Argentina. His areas of interest are Wesleyan theology and liberation theology. He has more than twenty articles published in journals of theology and social sciences and an essay in the collective book *Abajo los muros: Lecturas Wesleyanas contemporáneas* (2018), ed. Pedro Zavala. He is an ordained elder and superintendent in the Evangelical Methodist Church of Argentina.

Helmut Renders is professor at the School of Theology and the Department of Religion and secretary of the Wesley Study Center at the Methodist University of São Paulo, Brazil. He is an ordained elder in the Methodist Church of Brazil. He is also the general editor of the *Biblia de Estudo John Wesley* (2020), published in cooperation with the Brazilian Bible Society, and the author of the books *John Wesley e a luta abolicionista* (2019), *Coragem de pensar o bem: Princípios e passos* (revised and enlarged edition, 2019), and *El humano y su mundo en permanente transformación e la Iglesia siempre reformandose* (2019). He also has chapters in *No Religion but Social Religion: Liberating Wesleyan Theology* (2018), ed. Joerg Rieger, and *Abajo los muros: Lecturas Wesleyanas contemporáneas* (2018), ed. Pedro Zavala.

Joerg Rieger is Distinguished Professor of Theology, Cal Turner Chancellor's Chair in Wesleyan Studies, and the founding director of the Wendland-Cook Program in Religion and Justice at Vanderbilt University Divinity School. His most recent books include *Jesus vs. Caesar: For People Tired of Serving the Wrong God* (2018), *No Religion but Social Religion: Liberating Wesleyan Theology* (2018), and *Unified We Are a Force: How Faith and Labor Can Overcome America's Inequalities* (with Rosemarie Henkel-Rieger, 2016). He is an elder in the United Methodist Church.

Upolu Lumā Vaai is professor of theology and ethics and principal of the Pacific Theological College, Fiji. He is the Oceania Chair of the Oxford Institute of Methodist Theological Studies, member of the Education for Justice (E4J) expert committee of the United Nations Office on Drugs and Crimes (UNODC), Pacific coordinator for the G20 Interfaith Summit, and chief editor of the Pacific Relational Renaissance Series. His most recent coedited volumes are *Relational Hermeneutics: Decolonising the Mindset and the Pacific Itulagi* (with Aisake Casimira, 2017), and *The Relational Self: Decolonising Personhood in the Pacific* (with Unaisi Nabobo-Baba, 2017). He is an ordained minister of the Methodist Church in Samoa.

Index

www.ingramcontent.com/pod-product-compliance
Lightning Source LLC
LaVergne TN
LVHW030920080826
845145LV00013B/2977